fabjob *Guide to*

BECOME AN EVENT PLANNER

JAN L. RIDDELL, CAROL PALMATIER
AND PETER J. GALLANIS

FABJOB® GUIDE TO
BECOME AN EVENT PLANNER
by Jan L. Riddell, Carol Palmatier and Peter J. Gallanis

ISBN 1-894638-54-9

National Library of Canada Cataloguing in Publication Data

Riddell, Jan, 1953-
    FabJob guide to become an event planner / Jan L. Riddell, Carol Palmatier and Peter J. Gallanis.

Includes bibliographical references.
ISBN 1-894638-54-9

1. Special events industry—Vocational guidance. 2. Special events—Planning. I. Palmatier, Carol II. Gallanis, Peter J. III. Title.
GT3405.R53 2003   394.2'068   C2003-905619-8

About the Websites Mentioned in this Guide: Although we aim to provide the information you need within the guide, we have also included a number of websites because readers have told us they appreciate knowing about sources of additional information. (**TIP:** Don't include a period at the end of a web address when you type it into your browser.) Due to the constant development of the Internet, websites can change. Any websites mentioned in this guide are included for the convenience of readers only. We are not responsible for the content of any sites except FabJob.com.

FabJob.com
19 Horizon View Court
Calgary, Alberta, Canada T3Z 3M5

FabJob.com
4603 NE University Village #224
Seattle, Washington, USA 98105

To order books in bulk, phone 403-949-4980, ext. 1
To arrange an author interview, phone 403-949-4980, ext. 3

www.FabJob.com

About the Authors

Jan L. Riddell has been planning events for more than 15 years. Some of the events she has planned with public attendance include annual outdoor pancake breakfasts attended by over 2500 people, book launches and author readings, town hall forums, car rallies and sporting events. Jan's work with a national TV broadcaster provided opportunities to plan events like television show premieres and new season launches. Jan also plans corporate engagements like annual general meetings, industry open houses, incentive travel bonuses and dinners with high profile politicians and corporate leaders. As well as working with corporate and industry clients Jan has also planned family reunions, birthdays and weddings and anniversaries. Jan studied Event Meeting Management at George Brown College in Toronto and in addition to planning events also has an interior decorating company.

Carol Palmatier is a marketing and communications professional with 15 years' experience creating memorable events and programs. She has worked with leaders in business and industry, as well as small businesses and non-profit organizations including the American Lung Association, National Safety Council and Girl Scouts of the USA. Her most recent work includes planning special events for the Greater Brighton Chamber of Commerce near Detroit, where she coordinates southeast Michigan's largest golf outing and spearheads the annual Brighton Art Fest. She is also one of three managing partners in Four Points Editorial, a content creation and editing firm with offices in Florida, Detroit and San Diego. A graduate of The College of Saint Rose in Albany, New York, she received her degree in Public Communications in 1985. She has lived in New York, San Francisco and now resides with her family in Michigan. Community involvement includes volunteering for Habitat for Humanity and the Special Olympics.

Peter J. Gallanis is a veteran newspaper and magazine reporter. In the course of his duties for publications such as the *Chicago Tribune* and *DSN Retailing Today*, a nation-wide retail trade publication, Gallanis has covered a variety of events including new store openings, press conferences and trade shows. On a more personal side, he's coordinated his own events, including baby showers, dinner parties and children's birthday parties. Gallanis lives in Chicago's northwest suburbs with his beautiful wife Chriselda and children Alexander and Antonia.

Contents

1. Introduction

Congratulations on choosing a career as an event planner! You are embarking on a path full of fun, excitement, big challenges and end-less possibilities. Your job will vary from day to day, even minute to minute, and you'll enjoy the satisfaction of creating fabulous events that will be the talk of the town. You'll work hard and, if you do it right, you'll make it look easy.

Some people have a real knack for throwing parties, organizing group activities, and moving people in a common direction. If this describes you, this guide will help you take that natural talent and channel it into a lucrative and rewarding career in event planning. This book will pro-vide you with a step-by-step road map for reaching success in the world of events. So let's get started!

1.1 Welcome to Event Planning

An event planner is, quite simply, someone who organizes events. When you think of an "event" you may think of something spectacular, such as the:

- Academy Awards

- Mardi Gras

- Super Bowl

- Presidential Inauguration

- New Year's festivities in Times Square

- Any other major events we hear about or see on television

Event planners are needed for all these events. Event planners also work on thousands of smaller events. Any time people gather together for a purpose, someone is needed to oversee all the details to ensure the event happens and that it is a success. The event planner is the primary point of contact for coordinating the countless details, both large and small, that go into a successful gathering.

As you will discover in chapter 2, event planners may work on:

- social events (birthday parties, private dinner parties, family reunions, etc.)

- corporate events (company social events, board meetings, open houses, etc.)

- industry events (conferences, association meetings, trade shows, etc.)

- special events (festivals, parades, fashion shows, etc.)

Some event planners work on staff for businesses, organizations and associations, while others work in the hospitality industry in hotels and conference centers. Other employers include casinos, country clubs, theme parks, and public relations firms. (Chapter 4 has more information about employers.) Many experienced planners are independent consultants, working for clients on a per-project basis.

You will often see meeting planners mentioned as a distinct group. Meeting Planners plan conventions, conferences and seminars for professional organizations and businesses.

Event planners, on the other hand, cover a wider range of events. Wedding planners form another distinct category, and are covered in another FabJob guide, *The FabJob Guide to Become a Wedding Planner*. A variety of other job titles related to event planning can be found in section 4.1.2.

1.1.1 Event Planning as a Profession

You are entering a vibrant, growing and rather young industry. The Convention Industry Council estimates that there are between 250,000 and 450,000 professional planners in the U.S. alone. That number continues to expand as more top executives recognize this relatively new profession.

While event planning has been around since the beginning of recorded history, only during the last 15 to 20 years has the industry been recognized as a separate entity with a distinct skill set and body of knowledge.

According to a recent Meeting Outlook Survey commissioned by Meeting Professionals International (MPI), the number of professionally-planned meetings has increased each year. Yearly growth for meeting planning is projected to range from five percent for associations over the next few years to 15 percent for corporations. While growth is particularly hot during a strong economy, the MPI Foundation/GPJ Event Trends Report 2003 reported an increase in events in 2003 despite sluggish travel and economic trends.

Growth is expected to continue throughout 2004. According to a study published by *Special Events Magazine* in August, 2003, "80 percent of in-house corporate event planners predict that their company's spending on events in 2004 will be on par with or better than 2003 spending."

1.1.2 Benefits of this Career

A career in event planning offers many personal and professional rewards, including:

Recognition

Events involve people – usually large groups of people – and you'll fast become known as the person behind the scenes who gets the job done and makes sure everything is done flawlessly. Event planning is a great way to get to know your community, and will help you network with the movers and shakers in your town, your state, and even beyond.

Financial Reward

With the increased recognition of event planning as an industry, professionals in the field are seeing an increase in compensation in both the business and non-profit arenas. In fact, a salary survey published in the May 2002 issue of *The Meeting Professional* (MPI's monthly publication) states that the average salary for a professional planner is just over $60,000 a year, up from $54,000 in 2000.

Personal Satisfaction

If you've ever known the satisfaction that comes from working incredibly hard on a challenge and seeing outstanding results, you can understand why event planning can be so rewarding on a personal level. Financial and professional rewards are fine, but what a gift it is to find a career that pays you to have this much fun!

Flexibility

If you are looking for a job that will allow you some flexibility in setting your own schedule, event planning might be a good fit. Many smaller organizations and businesses can't afford a full-time event planner. And recent downsizing in some fields have left remaining staff maxed out in terms of their job responsibilities. This creates an opportunity for part-time or seasonal work rather than a rigid 9-to-5 routine.

> "I recently joined the staff of my local Chamber of Commerce as their event coordinator. The Chamber sponsors four major fundraising events each year. The job averages about 15 hours per week, but prior to each event the time commitment can be much greater. By taking this job, I am able to adjust my other client work and arrange vacation and travel time with my family – a perfect balance!"
> – Carol Palmatier

Independence

Because of the timely and transient nature of event planning, the field lends itself beautifully to independent consulting. If you've ever wanted to start your own business, this field offers some terrific opportunities. More detailed information on starting your own business as an event planner can be found in Chapter 5.

1.2 Inside this Guide

This book was written to help launch you into your new career by providing industry information, event planning guidelines, helpful hints on finding and getting work, and advice on starting your own event planning business.

Chapter 2 will explain in more detail the role of an event planner, and give you step-by-step guidance on planning an event – from the initial planning stage to the day of the event.

In Chapter 3, we'll outline the talents and skills you will need in order to be a smashing success as an event planner, and offer suggestions on how to develop those skills through formal and continuing education and self-study.

Chapter 4 focuses on Event Planning Jobs. You will discover who hires event planners, how to find out about job openings, how to prepare an effective resume and cover letter, and how to do well in an interview. You will even discover how to create your own job!

If you want to Start Your Own Business, you will find some good advice in chapter 5. You will find practical information on setting up your office and getting ready to open for business, including setting your fees. In chapter 6, you will discover practical tips for Getting Clients.

When you're finished with this guide you will know what step to take next and where to go from there. By applying what you learn here, it's just a matter of time before you'll be where you want to be… in an exciting career as an Event Planner!

2. What an Event Planner Does

Event planners have been compared to the man behind the curtain in *The Wizard of Oz*, a plate spinner in the circus or a juggler. The common thread in each description is that an event planner creates something fabulous out of the myriad details, all while making it look easy.

In this chapter, we will give you an overview of the types of services provided in several different event situations, outline the actual steps to planning an event, and give you sample documents and checklists you can use in your own work.

2.1 Services Provided by an Event Planner

So what exactly does an event planner do? Just as each event varies in its size, scope and complexity, so each job will differ. Depending on the event, you may be asked to do any number of different tasks, all with the end result of achieving a successful event.

The steps to planning an anniversary or bar mitzvah will obviously differ somewhat from the steps involved in the successful planning of a large convention or board meeting for a corporation. However, as different as those events are, many steps in the planning process are similar no matter what type of event you are planning. To illustrate, look at a few of the steps common to planning both an anniversary party and convention:

- client consultation (meeting with client)

- set budget

- choose date

- select venue (location)

- negotiate with and choose suppliers

- arrange transportation

- book blocks of hotel rooms for any out of town attendees

- arrange caterer and choose menu for dinner

- book entertainment, speakers or music provider

Of course, not all of the steps involved in planning an anniversary party are mirrored in planning a convention, but you can see in the above example that even though the purpose or end use of the item may not be the same, you will be responsible for set up and coordination of similar items. In the sections that follow, you will discover details about each of the steps involved in organizing an event.

However, although there are some similarities in planning different types of events, there are some differences depending on the type of event being planned. So this section provides an overview of different types of events, so you can decide if there are certain types that you would like to specialize in.

We've grouped the different kinds of events into four main categories – social events, corporate events, industry events, and special events – to give you an idea of exactly what might be required of you.

2.1.1 Social Events

You have probably, at one time or another, been involved in planning social events. Birthdays, baby showers, bar mitzvahs, dinner parties, weddings, reunions, and other events — odds are, you've not only been to many, but had a hand in helping to plan some of them.

As events become more sophisticated and guests become more demanding, individuals are turning to event planners, and in a big way. According to *Special Events Magazine*, event planners are forecast to earn 35 percent of their 2003 income from social clients.

Some event planners specialize in planning social events and prefer not to get involved in planning corporate or other events. Due to the sheer variety of social events, you can make a very good living on these events alone.   The following is a list of common social events you may be asked to undertake:

- anniversary parties

- baby showers

- bar or bat mitzvahs

- birthday parties

- child or adult baptism

- holiday dinners: Thanksgiving, Christmas, Easter

- holiday parties: Christmas, 4th of July, Canada Day

- housewarming

- neighborhood block parties

- reunions

- weddings

You'll likely be the calm in the storm of a family event, as emotions often run high on special occasions. Be friendly, be supportive, but don't be afraid to be firm when the hostess gets a little frantic or the guests decide to play pranks on the unsuspecting honorees. It will be up to you to maintain order and make sure everyone knows their role and exactly what's expected of them.

2.1.2 Corporate Events

As mentioned above, event planners often choose a particular type of event as their specialty, and corporate events are no exception. Many event planning companies prefer not to get involved in social events and will instead plan mostly corporate events. Some types of corporate events are:

- annual shareholder meetings

- board meetings

- client appreciation events

- company socials: holiday party, sporting event, car rally

- groundbreaking ceremony for construction of a new building

- incentive travel

- open houses

- new product launch

- press briefings

- staff training

- union events: meetings or family outings

With a sluggish economy and unpredictable world events having a dampening effect on corporate travel, planners are seeing an increase in e-conferencing as a cost-effective solution. Tel-events are becoming increasingly popular in large companies where participants hail from around the country or around the globe.

When working with a corporation, it is important to pay careful attention to the corporate culture. For example, employees of an Internet company celebrating their IPO are unlikely to respond well to a formal suit and tie affair, while a group of international financiers will probably not be comfortable at an indoor luau. While it's always good to give participants a shot of the unexpected, be careful that the event is relevant to the way they view their company.

2.1.3 Industry Events

Ah, conventions. To some, the very word conjures up images of rowdy businessmen in funny hats, roaming the hotel hallways in search of a good time. But that image of conventions is outdated, as industry events today are sophisticated affairs designed to inform, influence and form consensus on a specific issue or common topic. In addition to conventions, other industry-specific events include:

- association meetings

- conferences

- industry tradeshows

- public exhibitions: bridal fairs, auto shows, home shows

- symposiums

Conventions and symposiums are not open to public participation. The target audience for these events consists of those in the industry or those who service or support the industry. Tradeshows may or may not target their audience to only those in that particular industry. The first few days of these exhibitions may be set aside only for industry insiders, with the last day being open to the general public.

Public exhibitions are events where suppliers of related end-use products and services invite all interested community members to view the latest trends and offerings in their industries for a nominal entry fee. Most of these events will have an educational component to them and will involve speakers, experts, live demonstrations and product sales.

2.1.4 Special Events

The term "special event" can describe a broad range of affairs including sporting events like the Super Bowl, state fairs, major public events like Mardi Gras or New Year's Eve in Times Square. Some of these events will have very targeted audiences:

- award events

- book signings/author readings

- CD release parties

- charity fund-raisers

- children's festivals

- ethnic celebrations

- fashion shows

- holiday special events

- inauguration ball

- music festival

- parades — holiday, Mardi Gras, New Year's Day, Easter

- political forums or debates

- restaurant opening

- sporting events —car races, halftime show

- store grand opening

2.2 Preliminary Steps to Plan an Event

In this section, we'll go through the initial steps required to get from idea to successful affair. So roll up your sleeves... it's time to get to work!

2.2.1 Consult with the Client

You will work with clients whether you have your own event planning business or work full-time planning events for one company. As a corporate event planner, your "clients" will likely be other departments in the company. Here are a few examples:

- The Human Resources department asks you to organize the employee Christmas party

- The Marketing Department wants to hold a sales conference at a resort

- The President's Office asks you to organize a board meeting

In each case, you would consult with these internal clients – as you would with clients of your own event planning business – to determine what they want for the event.

At this initial meeting, you'll do more listening than talking, so pay careful attention to everything the client says. It might be helpful to record the meeting (get the client's permission first) or bring along an assistant or a partner who can take notes for you.

You can start out by asking the client to describe their vision for the event. Broad ideas are okay at this stage in the discussion — you will refine the vision as you move through the planning process. Questions such as the following will help you begin to visualize the event, and serve as the foundation for all the work to come. Think of this as the "big picture" overview.

- What kind of event do you want? (What is your vision for this event?)

- What do you hope to accomplish?

- When do you want to hold the event?

- Who is expected to attend? (What is the target audience?)

- What is the budget for the event?

At the end of the consultation, you should have a clear picture of what your client envisions for their event and be able to form a clear, concise "mission statement" or objective (see section 2.2.2).

Take some time at the end of the meeting to reiterate to the client your understanding of the event to make sure you are both on the same wavelength. This is usually an exciting meeting and a good opportunity for both you and the client to learn more about each other and how you will work together.

This is a good time to talk about who will be involved in the planning process, who will be the key decision makers, and how information should flow during the planning stage. Remember, as the event planner, it is your responsibility to take charge of the planning. Now is the time to eliminate as many roadblocks as you can before you reach them.

For example, if all decisions involving the budget have to be approved by someone in corporate accounting, find out how they need to be informed, what kind of lead time they need, and who is the best person to push it through. You don't want to be caught waiting for a check while your invitations languish in the printing office.

Also find out how much leeway you will have in the decision-making process. Some clients just want you to "handle it," while others will want to have input on the smallest detail, right down to the font on the cocktail napkins. Recognize this – and respect their right to be as involved as they want – but make it clear that turnaround time is critical in event planning. It may be fun for the client to linger for hours over a linen catalog, but a busy event planner has to set a firm time frame in which decisions need to be made.

> **TIP:** You can help this process along by narrowing the choices down to two or three at each stage. This way, the client still retains the right to choose, but you'll already have done the leg work and made the decision that much easier.

While this initial meeting is still fresh in your mind, **summarize** the discussion in writing and send a copy to the client. If at all possible, do this the same day or the day after the meeting. Miscommunication at this stage of the game can be detrimental to an event, so be sure you both clearly see the same big picture.

For more information about client consultations, see section 6.5.2 of this guide.

2.2.2 Set Objectives

The best and most successful events have a clear purpose or objective. Some are obvious — for instance, a wedding's purpose is to publicly celebrate a marriage. Others are not so apparent. A community festival's outward purpose might be to provide an exciting day of family activities for the locals, but its broader objective might be to boost the area's image as a tourist destination.

Event planners can take a lesson from good management techniques and use the S.M.A.R.T. method, a well-recognized model for setting strategic objectives. To be S.M.A.R.T., your objectives should be:

- **Specific**: What is the specific result of your event? (Instead of just saying you want your charity fashion show to "raise money," state a specific amount you want to raise.)

- **Measurable**: Can the outcome be measured in a reliable way? (For example, if you want your event to "increase public awareness," how will you measure whether or not public awareness has actually increased?)

- **Attainable**: Given staffing, budget, timing and other restraints, is the objective attainable?

- **Relevant**: Do the people involved have the authority, the skill and the resources needed to meet the objective? And is the objective important to the organization?

- **Time-Based**: Is there a start and end point to the objective?

Let's look at an example. Consider a non-profit organization that is attempting to raise a significant amount of money for a new museum collection. The initial goal might be to have a fund-raiser that draws a large number of guests and raises a lot of money. If we apply the S.M.A.R.T. principle to this general goal, our objective might be:

The New Art Foundation will host a black tie silent auction and celebrity dinner. The goal is 1,000 attendees, 200 new members, and $80,000 raised for the Bradford collection, a new group of work to be permanently housed at the NAF Center. The event will be held six months from now at the Oak Manor House, and will be coordinated by foundation staff and an independent planning consultant. Expenses for the event will be included in this year's foundation budget.

Examining the objective, we can see that it meets the SMART criteria:

- **Specific**: 1,000 guests, 200 new members, $80,000 raised

- **Measurable**: head count, new member application, funds raised from auction and admission

- **Attainable**: coordinated by staff and consultant, adequate time to plan, money included in foundation budget

- **Relevant**: staff will have the ability to make this event a reality, and the event itself is in line with the principles and mission of the New Art Foundation

- **Time-Based**: mid-June; one day event means distinct end date

Setting S.M.A.R.T. objectives will not only make the planning easier, but will help measure the success of the event and create a positive experience for all involved.

> **TIP:** After defining the purpose or mission statement, keep it visible by summarizing it and using it as a header on all written documentation, including correspondence with all of the event's stakeholders (people of primary interest).

2.2.3 Choose a Date

It is in this stage that the preferred date of the event should be decided upon. Clients will often – but not always – come with a date in mind for the event. If they don't, it will be your job to help pick a suitable date. However, whether this responsibility has been left up to you or not, you need to consider the following before choosing the date or accepting the client.

Consider your availability. Don't set yourself up to fail by accepting a client, knowing that you cannot possibly do a stellar job due to time constraints or a conflict with another event. Allow yourself enough time for follow-up and rest after the end of one event before tackling another. Always bring your up-to-date calendar with you to any meetings and be diligent in recording events you are already committed to.

Consider other events in the area. What other events are being held in the chosen (preferred) city or location that could interfere or make it difficult to secure wanted facilities or services (Mardi Gras in New Orleans, for example)?

Consider the season and usual weather in the chosen location. You will want to avoid hurricane, avalanche or other severe storm seasons when choosing a locale. Also, choose a "season appropriate" date for the desired activities.

Consider your suppliers. Are your usual preferred suppliers available during the time of the event? Once you've built a list of solid, reputable suppliers, it can be a little scary to take a chance on someone new for an important event. Try to ensure your trusted suppliers can accommodate the event.

Consider other company-related events. Avoid conflicts with other company events or busy times of year. For instance, if the company is a book publisher, you will want to steer clear of the annual Book Expo America happenings, since many employees will likely be tied up with that event. If your clients are financial planners, avoid planning something during tax season.

Consider other holidays. Try to avoid religious, civic, or statutory holidays when prices could be well above normal and venues are swamped with other tourists.

Consider your time needs. Determine if there is enough time before the chosen or preferred date to enable you to accomplish all of the necessary details.

2.2.4 Decide Who to Invite

One essential piece of information you need before you proceed with any of the planning stages of an event is this: Who is your target audience? This holds true no matter what type of event you are planning, from corporate meetings or conferences and tradeshows to Grandma Smith's 90th birthday party. If you don't know who you're trying to reach, you could waste precious time and money reaching the wrong audience. Here's an example:

> Referring back to our New Art Foundation objectives, you would of course invite current members of the foundation and its donors. You might also target local artists and arts patrons. You will also want to invite your membership prospect list, as well as members and staff of similar foundations and arts organizations. Don't neglect college and university VIPs, and of course any relevant elected officials and key city staffers.

Your client needs to give you an idea of who they want to attend their event before you can begin to formulate a plan to attract the target audience or plan activities. You will need to know the following:

- How many people would the client like to invite?

- Will spouses or families also attend?

- What are the demographics of the target audience (e.g. gender, median age, ethnic background, income bracket)?

- What interests do they share (recreational activities, such as golf, tennis or skiing or cultural opportunities)?

- What payback does the client expect?

- Where are the attendees coming from (this is very important to note, as translators or a quick lesson in another country's customs may be necessary)?

Number of Attendees

Until you know approximately how many people are to be invited, it will be very difficult to decide the type and size of a venue, or the transportation needs and amount of food required. If the event is a recurring one, records from previous years will help you determine approximate numbers. If this is the first year the event is being held, there are standard accepted ways of estimating numbers.

Generally, industry insiders will tell you that if the event is privately hosted and the guests are known to the host, 25 percent of the people invited will not show up, even if they have responded that they will attend. When guests are paying to attend the event, the number of no-shows drops to approximately 15 percent.

If the event is advertised and open to the general public, it will be harder to ascertain numbers of attendees. One effective tool is to use the previous year's attendance figures as a general guideline and then add to or subtract from those figures based on such things as recent media publicity.

Once you have an idea who is expected to attend the event, you will be in a much better position to choose food and beverages, entertainment, a theme and the venue.

2.2.5 Create Your Theme

The most memorable events have a cohesive theme that runs throughout, from initial publicity to printed invitations to decor and right through to the entertainment and final applause. An appropriate, exciting and consistent theme is one of the best ways to leave your audience wanting more.

Coming up with a creative theme can seem like a daunting task to a new event planner, but once you get started you'll see this is one of the best ways to show off your creative side and a lot of fun.

One of the biggest advantages of a strong theme is its usefulness in helping you make decisions throughout the event process. For example, if you decide that the theme for the Winter Ball should be an Evening in Las Vegas, you have already narrowed down the field for venues, entertainment, menu choices and the like. And you'll have a ready source for inspiration when it comes time to choose graphics, create publicity, decide on décor, etc. Once a theme has been decided on, print materials such as invitations, banners, place cards, brochures, advertising and websites can be designed.

So, where do you get ideas for a great theme? Everywhere!

Brainstorm

Hold a brainstorming session with the event stakeholders, during which everyone is encouraged to throw out their wildest and most off-the-wall ideas. Write everything down, and encourage free discussion on how a theme would develop. You can build great momentum by letting people throw out their ideas and build off others. Tell participants not to be afraid to think outside the box. Once you've hit on a theme that works, you can always revise it to meet your objectives.

Events Industry

If you're still having trouble coming up with a theme check out what Event Planners in other cities or states are up to, but be careful to make any idea uniquely your own — don't simply copy a previous event. You'll want your event to have a mark of its own, not seem like "been there, done that."

Among the many great industry sources for ideas are Special Event Source at **www.specialeventsource.com** (click on "Idea Center" at the bottom of the page) and *Special Events Magazine* at **www. specialevents.com**. Stumps, at **www.stumpsprom.com** and **www.shindigz.com**, sells theme kits, and can provide a springboard for your own ideas.

Current Events and Trends

Read magazines like *Entertainment Weekly* to keep up with what's hot in TV shows, current events, and trends. Here are some event ideas based on what's hot:

- Reality based TV shows have turned the entertainment world on it's ear and given event planners a wealth of new ideas. Ideas based on *Survivor, The Amazing Race,* or *The Mole* can turn a dull event into an exciting one. Take *Survivor* for instance. A corporate team-building event could include crazy challenges for participants loosely based on the real challenges on the show (without the bug-eating, of course). Drink stations (portable bars) could be set up inside grass huts built for the event and the whole room could be wired to play jungle sounds. The walls could be decorated with hanging vines and instead of traditional tables and chairs, hammocks, hanging chairs and rough-hewn logs would serve as places to sit.

- Many parties are held on the same night as the Oscars are handed out, with big screen TVs showing all the action. Guests come all a glitter in the latest fashion or dressed as a character from their favorite movie. Movies like *Chicago* and *Lord of the Rings* presented lots of opportunity for dress-up.

2.2.6 Set the Event Agenda

You've chosen the date and the theme, roughed up a guest list and created smart objectives. Now it's time to set the agenda for the event. Whether your event is an hour-long awards dinner or a three-day festival, it's important to lay out the entire schedule. Include adequate time for registration, socializing, speakers, awards, meal service, etc.

This is a great time to do a "visualization" of the event. Run through the entire program from start to finish, making notes of any materials, services, room setups and special arrangements you might need. This will help you create the list of vendors to contact and tasks to be done. We'll go into this in more detail in the next section.

2.3 Get Organized

As a successful event planner, you will develop a variety of organizational tools that will help you keep track of all the many details involved in all the events you will be organizing. In this section of the guide you will find a selection of samples to help you get started. As you start working with clients on actual events, you can adapt and customize these tools and techniques to find the ones that work best for you.

2.3.1 Establish Event Committees

There may be the odd occasion when you will do all the planning and organizing of an event yourself. However, few events are a "one person show." In most cases you will work with a group of people who are expected to help make the event a success.

Choose a select group of key people from these stakeholders and form an Event Committee. You'll be on the committee, but don't name yourself as the Chairperson. That role should go to someone with a lot of respect in the organization, someone with the ability to make decisions and build consensus. The Chairperson should also be a good motivator and help focus the work of the rest of the committee.

Assign specific items to each committee member according to their expertise. For example, for a non-profit fundraiser, the Chairperson might be a board member who happens to work for one of the major event sponsors. This person will use their clout to solicit other corporate sponsors and partners.

Other committee members can come from within the staff, membership and volunteer core of the organization. Consider asking vendors with whom the group does a lot of business to be on the committee. They may be more willing to cut you a good discount on the invitations and programs, which can really help your bottom line.

Your committee should meet fairly frequently, and each committee member should present an update of their specific task or tasks. Make sure no one is falling behind, and diplomatically offer to find someone to help them if it looks like they need a hand. Remember, it is your responsibility to ensure that all these balls stay in the air.

Document everything, and make your notes neat and organized. A large binder with tabs for each item is an excellent idea. By carefully documenting all details, you'll not only make your own job easier, but you'll ensure a good event for your client. One event planner who contributed to this guide said: "I use the "hit by a truck" approach. If I am hit by a truck tomorrow, someone else should be able to pick up the binder and carry on with little difficulty."

Before each meeting, touch base with the Chairperson and decide on an agenda. There will be a lot of information to share – and no one likes long rambling meetings – so make every effort to stick to it. A sample agenda might look like this:

Sample Meeting Agenda

New Art Foundation Fundraiser

Committee Meeting
November 2, 2003
4:00 p.m.

1. Welcome
2. Chairperson's report
3. Committee reports
   - venue
   - food and beverage
   - entertainment
   - tickets
   - door prizes
   - silent auction donations
4. Budget update
5. Staff report
6. New Business
7. Next meeting/adjournment

After the meeting, send minutes (a report of what happened) to all committee members, and copies to any other interested stakeholders.

2.3.2 Timeline Schedule

Creating a timeline schedule is an important step to ensure the success of your event. Ideally, most events will start with a plan at least six months before the event, while larger-scale events can begin at least a year in advance. (Of course some events are planned within weeks, while others – such as major conventions – can take years of planning.) Base your own event's timeline on factors such as:

- the size of event

- the location

- the time of year

- the number of people involved in planning

You can use the sample timeline below as a starting point to assist you in planning. Your own timeline will of course vary depending on the particular event you are organizing.

For example, if people need to make travel arrangements or book time off work to attend your event, you may want to invite them months ahead of time. Whereas if the event is one that people are likely to decide at the last minute to attend, you might send your invitations within a week or two of the event.

After you have prepared the timeline, you will develop a detailed "Critical Path" (covered in section 2.3.3) which outlines specific tasks, deadlines, and responsibilities.

Once you have created a timeline for your event, you should then either write down the items to be handled in a daytimer or on a calendar, insert the information into a simple Excel or similar spreadsheet program, or put it into an electronic organizer such as a Palm Pilot. Another alternative is to use event planning software, which is covered in section 5.2.3 of this guide.

Sample Timeline

6 Months Before

_____   Set event goals and objectives
_____   Determine guest list
_____   Choose date
_____   Select location
_____   Outline agenda
_____   Set budget
_____   Decide on theme

3 Months Before

_____   Design, print and mail invitations
_____   Launch promotion and publicity campaign
_____   Choose menu and decorations
_____   Hire photographers
_____   Contract with entertainers
_____   Choose A/V supplier
_____   Make travel arrangements
_____   Book any accommodations
_____   Prepare a detailed agenda
_____   Purchase supplies, awards, gifts and incidentals

1 Month Before

_____   Reconfirm all contracts and reservations
_____   Finalize menu and serving style
_____   Continue publicity
_____   Finalize setup details
_____   Assign tasks for day of event
_____   Arrange for necessary security

2 Weeks Before

_____   Prepare final attendee list
_____   Check with venue for last minute site details
_____   Schedule dress rehearsal

The Week Before

_____ Give final headcount to vendors, caterer and venue
_____ Prepare name tags, registration packets and materials
_____ Prepare final payments for suppliers
_____ Prepare gifts for guests and speakers
_____ Hold rehearsal

Day of the Event

_____ Finalize registration setup and review procedures with staff
_____ Set up signs, posters, room markers
_____ Arrange displays or exhibits
_____ Distribute and collect evaluation forms
_____ Pay suppliers and vendors, and distribute tips
_____ Clean up and tear down
_____ Return any rented equipment

Adding Detail

As you start developing your own checklists, it is a good idea to include as much detail as possible for each item. For example under "Assign tasks for day of event" you would list the specific tasks that need to be assigned, such as:

_____ Driving (picking up at airport, taking to event, to lunch, back to plane)
_____ Supervising set-up of groundbreaking site
_____ Leading briefing session with speakers
_____ Greeting people at entrance to event site, distributing name-tags, seating
_____ Ushering speakers during event, handing them shovels and hard hats
_____ Assisting media to arrange interviews and take photos
_____ Supervising set-up of luncheon site
_____ Greeting people as they arrive at luncheon

The Professional Convention Management Association offers a number of checklists at their website, including a very detailed (6 pages) Planning Checklist for a convention. Visit **www.pcma.org** and do a search for "checklists."

Once you've developed the checklist, assign target dates to each item. Many professional planners recommend working backwards from your event date.

For example, if you want the RSVPs in one month before the event, then plan to mail the invitations four weeks prior to the RSVP date. That means you should get the invitations to the printers at least two weeks before the mailing date. And so on. By working backwards, you won't have to play catch-up in the busy weeks leading up to your bash.

Sample Checklist for Day of Event

The following checklist is for a groundbreaking ceremony and luncheon. It shows the level of detail that can assist in ensuring your events run as smoothly as possible. In this scenario, the groundbreaking is for a manufacturing plant in a rural community, and company representatives from Denver will need to be flown in to the community where the event is happening.

Groundbreaking Site

8:00 - 9:00 a.m.   Site set up (refer to diagram)
_____ Support staff arrive at set-up location
_____ Tent put up at 8:30 a.m. (sides to be up or down depending on weather)
_____ 60 chairs set up in tent, room for aisles and standing room at back
_____ Sound sytem set up (do a test to ensure mic and tape player work)
_____ Lighting set up throughout tent
_____ Heater set up at side of tent
_____ Banner put up
_____ Front of tent set up
　　　_____ Microphone and podium in centre at front
　　　_____ Podium sign placed on podium with velcro dots
　　　_____ 5 chairs for speakers
　　　_____ Easel with artist's rendition
　　　_____ Flowers
　　　_____ 3 shovels with bows tied on them
　　　_____ 3 hard hats
　　　_____ Marker for digging spot

    ____ Entrance to tent set up
        ____ Table with skirting
        ____ Two chairs and waste basket at table
        ____ Nametags in alphabetical order on table
        ____ Easel with artist's rendition
        ____ Flowers

10:00 a.m.   ____ Charter plane from Denver arrives
    ____ Denver people picked up at airport and brought to building
    ____ Signs directing people to site are put up by now
    ____ If it is cold and raining, start heater

10:30 a.m.   ____ Briefing session at administrative building
    ____ Distribute name tags to staff and speakers
    ____ Run through what will happen during event

11:00 a.m.   ____ Staff to greet guests arrives at entrance to site
    ____ Staff to greet guests arrives at tent
    ____ Photographer arrives at tent
    ____ Start music (low volume)

11:15 a.m.   ____ This is the time invitation asks guests to arrive
    ____ Turn off heater
    ____ Greet guests as they arrive
    ____ Hand out nametags
    ____ Hand out information kits
    ____ Assist with seating if needed

11:30 a.m.   ____ Turn off music
    ____ MC announces event is about to begin, asks people to take seats
    ____ 3 speakers ushered to front
    ____ MC speaks
        ____ Welcomes and thanks all for attending
        ____ Explains what will happen
        ____ Gives a very brief overview
        ____ Introduces and thanks each speaker
    ____ MC announces sod turning will now take place
    ____ Sod-turning
        ____ 3 speakers move to marked site
        ____ Support staff hand shovels and hard hats to each of the 3 speakers
        ____ Photographers get in place
        ____ MC invites 3 to "dig in"
        ____ The 3 stick shovels in ground and pose, scoop a little dirt

11:45 a.m.	_____	Conclusion of event

_____ The 3 stay standing where they are

_____ MC says "this concludes formal part of groundbreaking"

_____ MC invites media to stay for interviews

12:00 p.m.	_____	Speakers led to ground transportation to go to luncheon

Luncheon Site

11:30 a.m.	_____	Luncheon support staff arrive at Civic Centre to supervise set-up

_____ Ensure proper room layout (see diagram)

_____ Help Civic Centre staff if necessary

_____ Test microphone, tape player, and overhead projector

_____ Put up banner

_____ Put sign on podium

_____ Set out name tags

_____ Put on music (low volume)

_____ Put small gift at each place setting

12:00 p.m.   _____   Guests start to arrive (be prepared for earlier arrivals too)

_____   Greet guests and give nametags if they want one

_____   Obtain names of guests as they arrive

_____   Show guests where to hang up coats

_____   Tell guests beverages are available

12:15 p.m.   _____   Announce beginning of buffet service

_____   Meals served to head table

1:00 p.m.   _____   Coffee, tea, and desert service begin

_____   Event planner gives MC a list of guests to acknowledge

1:15 p.m.   _____   Presentations

_____   MC speaks

_____   Welcomes everyone

_____   Acknowledges special guests

_____   Introduces luncheon speaker

_____   Speaker gives 10 minute talk

_____   MC thanks speaker and invites Mayor to podium

_____   Mayor presents gift to President

_____   Company President thanks Mayor

_____   MC invites people to remain for coffee

2:15 p.m.   _____   Denver people on charter flight leave for airport

2:45 p.m.   _____   Charter flight leaves airport for Denver

2.3.3 Critical Path

Unlike a timeline schedule, a Critical Path (or Assignment of Tasks) lists each of the tasks that needs to be accomplished, who is responsible for it, and the deadline by which it will be done. A Critical Path is used as a guide map for the event, to assist when delegating responsibilities, and show whether you are on track.

You can create a critical path with event planning software such as those described in section 5.2.3, or a basic program such as Excel. In the sample Critical Path that appears on the CD-ROM (included at the back of this book), all items that need to be accomplished for the successful completion of this event are listed. It includes the following columns:

- An "action by" column allows for each task to be assigned to a specific person and a specific organization.

- A due date column gives you a quick glance at the status of a task, and the column for comments or special concerns can be altered as circumstances change.

- You can also include a column to record when an item has been completed or for a quick scan to see how the planning is proceeding. Completed tasks could be indicated with "C" in the final column.

2.3.4 Budgets

Creating a budget (and sticking to it!) is an important ingredient in a successful event. Once you have created your timeline schedule and critical path, you can come up with a list of estimated expenses. Your expenses will of course include such items as venue rental, food, transportation, accommodations, audio-visual equipment, printed materials, and gifts.

> **TIP:**   You can find out how much a particular item is likely to cost by getting price quotes from vendors. (See section 2.5 for information on vendors.)

You will also need to include your own fee, and the client may want to include any staff time they spend on the event as an expense.

When planning the budget, don't forget to include your potential revenue to offset the costs. For example, is the event a fundraiser? Is it a convention or conference that should aim to cover its own expenses? Attendance fees, sales of related materials, donations, ticket sales and sponsorship can all be good ways to raise revenue.

Below you will see a Sample Budget for the groundbreaking event described earlier, followed by an Event Planning Budget Form you can use to start budgeting for your own events.

After the event you should compare actual expenses and revenues to your budgeted amounts. Not only will this help in determining whether your objectives were met, it may assist in budgeting for future events.

Sample Budget

Groundbreaking Ceremony Estimated Expenses

Groundbreaking Site

Tent	400.00	
Chairs	125.00	
Banner	383.00	
Podium sign	45.00	
Lights	50.00	
Flowers	50.00	
Shovels	51.86	
Subtotal		$1,104.86

Luncheon Expenses

Lunch	950.00	
Rental of Civic Centre	500.00	
Floral centerpieces	300.00	
Gifts for dignitaries (6 plaques)	810.00	
Gifts for guests (150 mini shovels)	1,535.00	
Information kit folders	150.00	
Printing of Fact Sheet	200.00	
Podium sign	45.00	
Subtotal		$4,590.00

Other Expenses

Services of Event Planner	9,000.00	
Long distance	100.00	
Printing of invitations	130.83	
Courier charges for invitations	200.00	
Delivery of boxes to site	320.00	
Photographer	291.00	
Sound system	934.56	
Charter plane	3,000.00	
Event Planner's travel	367.18	
Rental of van/minibus	160.00	
News release distribution service	640.00	
Subtotal		$15,143.57

TOTAL ESTIMATED EXPENSES $20,838.43
(taxes not included)

The form below lists items you may wish to include in the budget for your own event. Because each event is different, there will likely be items on this list that you will not need for your events, and others that you will want to add, or put into different categories.

Event Planning Budget Form

EXPENSES	Estimated	Actual
Site		
Venue or tent rental	_____	_____
Tables and chairs	_____	_____
Meals and beverages	_____	_____
Tableware rental	_____	_____
Staging	_____	_____
Audiovisual equipment	_____	_____
Decorations	_____	_____
Flowers	_____	_____
Other:		
_____	_____	_____
_____	_____	_____
_____	_____	_____
_____	_____	_____
Program		
Musicians	_____	_____
Speakers	_____	_____
Celebrities	_____	_____
Entertainers	_____	_____
Gifts	_____	_____
Awards	_____	_____
Activities (e.g. golf)	_____	_____
Other:		
_____	_____	_____
_____	_____	_____
_____	_____	_____
_____	_____	_____

Event Planning Budget Form (continued)

EXPENSES	Estimated	Actual

Printing and Promotion

	Estimated	Actual
Printing invitations	_____	_____
Mailing invitations	_____	_____
Banners and signs	_____	_____
Printing tickets	_____	_____
Event programs	_____	_____
Name tags	_____	_____
Shipping materials to venue	_____	_____
Advertising	_____	_____
Distribution of news release	_____	_____
Media kits	_____	_____
Long distance telephone	_____	_____
Other:		
_____	_____	_____
_____	_____	_____
_____	_____	_____
_____	_____	_____

Personnel

	Estimated	Actual
Event Planner	_____	_____
Staff salaries and benefits	_____	_____
Registration	_____	_____
Photographer	_____	_____
Bartenders	_____	_____
Security staff	_____	_____
Set-up and tear down	_____	_____
Other:		
_____	_____	_____
_____	_____	_____
_____	_____	_____

Event Planning Budget Form (continued)

EXPENSES	Estimated	Actual
Travel		
Airline tickets	_____	_____
Hotel rooms	_____	_____
Ground transportation	_____	_____
Other:		
_____	_____	_____
_____	_____	_____
_____	_____	_____
Other Expenses		
Insurance	_____	_____
Taxes	_____	_____
Legal services	_____	_____
Office supplies	_____	_____
Other:		
_____	_____	_____
_____	_____	_____
_____	_____	_____

REVENUE	Estimated	Actual
Registration fees	_____	_____
Ticket sales	_____	_____
Donations	_____	_____
Sponsorships	_____	_____
Advertising in event program	_____	_____
Other:		
_____	_____	_____
_____	_____	_____
_____	_____	_____

2.3.5 Crisis and Backup Planning

No event – no matter how well-planned and well-run – is immune to the occasional crisis or disaster. Take, for example, the Saturn car company of Spring Hill, Tennessee.

In 1994, Saturn planned a wonderful weekend event for its customers, complete with entertainment, barbecue, factory tours and family amusements for 38,000 guests. In the middle of the party, a large tornado tore through the site, wreaking havoc and nearly causing panic.

Thanks in large part to some level-headed staff and a good emergency plan, injuries were dealt with quickly, guests were kept calm and well-informed, and the entire party joined forces in a massive cleanup effort. In fact, Saturn has been cited for excellence in crisis and contingency planning by industry professionals.

Disasters and crises can range from relatively small (the keynote speaker's plane is delayed due to bad weather) to huge and seemingly insurmountable, like the Saturn tornado. A good event planner will be able to think on his or her feet for the small stuff, and have a solid crisis plan in place for dealing with the biggies. You can't possibly expect to plan for every type of crisis, but a little advance planning will go a long way to ensure that you can handle whatever comes your way.

Prior to the day of the event, put together a crisis response team and develop a plan. Include venue staff and local emergency response officials. Decide who will handle communications with the emergency personnel, the press, the attendees and other key groups, and do a run-through of a staged emergency. It's a good idea to give everyone on the team a laminated card with contact names and numbers, and make sure mobile phones or walkie-talkies are available, charged and in good working order.

Maintenance Emergencies

If your event takes place in a hotel or convention facility you should discuss emergency plans with the Director of Sales and Maintenance Engineer. They should provide you with a contact at the site who will take care of any emergency or maintenance issues. If your event is being held in a private hall, find out who in their organization is responsible for these types of issues and ask for someone to be available during your event. In your contact list, keep numbers of 24-hour locksmiths, plumbers and electricians.

> **TIP:** Make sure you get written permission and permits squared away as early in the process as possible. Outdoor events taking place in public areas like parks will need to be cleared through the city, and they may have specific requirements regarding sanitation, setup, parking, security and traffic flow. Understand local ordinances and procedures, and never, ever, ever assume that you are in compliance. When in doubt, ask. Then get it in writing!

Medical Emergencies

When planning a large outdoor festival or sporting event, it is advisable to have first aid personnel on hand for emergencies. Festival goers may suffer from heat stroke (or hypothermia in a cold location), minor or major cuts, sunburn or food poisoning. It's a good idea to include in your rental items a tent that can be used to shelter people from the sun or cold while receiving treatment for minor injuries.

Discuss options and get advice from your local ambulance volunteer force or contracted service providers. Be sure to include the local hospital, emergency line and non-emergency police number in your list of contacts.

Demonstrations or Other Confrontations

Although it sounds far-fetched that you will ever run into this circumstance, you should be prepared for it to happen. An example of an event that could bring unwanted confrontations is a fashion show. Animal rights activists may demonstrate against the clothing designer who includes fur in the runway line-up.

If you are involved in planning an event that could have some controversy attached to it, you should have uniformed security staff on hand to handle the situation. If the event is a large conference of international leaders, you should make contact with local law enforcement officers.

Weather

Extreme weather happens and it frequently happens unexpectedly. If you are planning an event for a storm-prone area, you might want to investigate acquiring insurance against extreme weather conditions.

2.3.6 The Rehearsal

We are all familiar with rehearsals for social events, especially weddings. The rehearsal is a dry run-through of the agenda for the main event, and gives the participants a chance to work out logistical details and ask questions about procedures, protocol and programs. Rehearsals are just as important for business and professional events, and should include staff working the event, key committee members, and, if possible, speakers and presenters or their representatives.

During the rehearsal, you'll want to check the following:

- **Registration:** Once the lobby is filled with guests, will the registration table block the flow of traffic? Do you have all the supplies you need, like pens, staplers, extra name tags, etc.?

- **Staging:** Are there stairs leading up to the stage? Can the speakers maneuver them with ease? How about podium height? Sufficient microphone stands? Do the potted palm trees block the audience's view of the speaker's slides?

- **Timing:** How long does it take for the award recipient to reach the stage? (In a large, crowded room, this might take a good deal longer than you imagine.)

- **Food service:** Is there ample room for wait staff to negotiate the crowd? How about the flow in and out of the kitchen area?

- **Participants:** Do all the speakers and presenters have a detailed copy of the program? Do they know their cue? Where can they look for a cue from a staff person? If VIPs require dressing rooms, have you timed the walk to the stage?

These are just a few of the questions that will be answered once you do a rehearsal of your event. Take notes and make sure any last minute details are ironed out before you hit the event for real.

2.4 Venues

If you work as an event planner for a facility such as a hotel, resort, convention center, or private club, this is one step you won't usually have to worry about. For other event planners, one of the most enjoyable parts of planning an event is coming up with a venue that shows off your creativity and fits the theme of the event.

The success of an event can be determined in large part to the facility or venue that it is held at. Imagine a rodeo being held in the ballroom of a swanky hotel, or a dinner for some traveling dignitary at a smoky rock-n-roll bar and you can see that selecting the correct venue is very important. That's not to say that you can't get creative and think outside the box when choosing a venue, but it should be appropriate for the client.

2.4.1 Finding a Venue

You have many choices for a venue. Here are some possibilities:

- Atrium of large building

- Client's place of business

- Community center

- Convention center

- Cruise ship or houseboat

- Golf and country club

- Guest Ranch

- Historical site

- Hotel

- Library meeting room

- Park or campground

- Planetarium

- Resort

- Restaurant

- Rooftop patio

- Sports complex

- Theatre

- University campuses

- Zoo or other outdoor attraction

To choose the right venue, it is important for the event planner to understand the special needs of each group of attendees. For example, if you have been hired to find a venue for a couples relationship weekend retreat perhaps a pastoral setting would fit better than an uptown urban one.

Finding Venues in Other Cities

Local Convention and Visitors Bureaus, Chambers of Commerce and hotel chains have resources available to event planners to evaluate potential sites. Check out the World Chamber of Commerce Directory at **www.chamberofcommerce.com** to find a branch near you.

OfficialTravelGuide.com lets you do a search by city. Type the city in the search box and you will get a link to the local convention and visitors bureau.

2.4.2 Space Requirements

To choose a facility, you will need to know how much physical space will be required. Once a preliminary agenda has been set, the number of rooms required for the event can be estimated. For example, if you are organizing a convention, is exhibit space required? In addition to meeting rooms will you need breakout rooms, special lounge areas, hospitality rooms or spouse/guest/children program rooms?

When determining your space needs, it helps to know what types of room set-ups you prefer. Sample room set-ups appear on the facing page.

Room Set-Ups

THEATER STYLE

This set-up is rows of chairs without tables. It is not good for note-taking. Avoid putting chairs right next to each other, and make sure there's enough room between rows for people to get in and out easily. Put chairs into a semi-circle or chevron set-up to create a greater connection among participants and with the presenter.

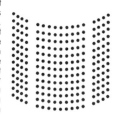

CLASSROOM STYLE

Sometimes referred to as "schoolroom style," this set-up involves rows of tables and chairs. Depending on the number of participants and the length of the table, there may be 2 to 4 people seated at each table. Make sure people have elbow room and room for writing, if needed.

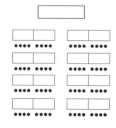

CHEVRON

Also known as "herringbone style" or "v-shaped," this set-up involves angling tables towards the front of the room. This creates more eye contact and a greater connection among the group.

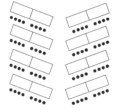

RECEPTIONS

For large receptions, you can minimize line-ups and crowding by putting several "stations" for food or drinks in different parts of the room. Use signs to direct people to different stations to avoid having people crowd the one closest to the entrance.

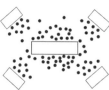

BANQUET

Banquets are best arranged with round tables seating 6 to 10 at each table. (A similar set-up, known as "cluster" is good for meetings that involve a lot of interacting in small groups.) Avoid long tables at banquets unless it's absolutely necessary because it reduces the opportunity for informal interaction.

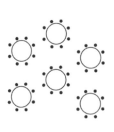

BOARD OF DIRECTORS

This a common set-up for small meetings. Avoid long rows of tables which make it difficult for participants to see everyone else.

HOLLOW SQUARE

This is a good set-up for small meetings. It allows greater eye contact with other participants than a long table, but is not good for showing audio-visuals.

HORSESHOE

Also known as "U-shape," this set-up works well with small groups of 24 or fewer. Participants can see everyone else, and the presenter can move freely throughout the room.

E-SHAPE

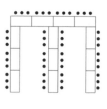

This set-up is a variation on the U-shape, which is commonly used to accommodate more people. However, it does not allow everyone to easily see all the other participants.

T-SHAPE

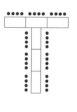

This set-up is sometimes used for small meetings. If more work space is needed, the center row can be double tables.

You can get free professional advice by speaking with staff in the sales or catering offices of venues you are considering using. They are experts on planning events in their facilities, and they can advise you on how much space you will need, based on the planned activities and number of participants.

Helpful Hints for Evaluating Space Needs

- A room laid out in theater style (chairs only), will allow you to fit at least twice as many people into a room as classroom style (tables and chairs). For theatre style choose a room that allows about 10 square feet per participant. For classroom style, the room should have about 20 square feet per participant (e.g. a 600 square foot room for 30 people).

- Allow 5 to 10 square feet per person for stand-up receptions. Make sure to have tables arranged around the room for people to deposit empty drink glasses and dishes. Also include space for bars and bartenders away from entrance and exit area.

- Banquet rooms should allow for 10 square feet per person (not including head tables and dance floors, if necessary). Allow space for food service areas and clear pathways for food servers.

2.4.3 Creating an RFP

While you can certainly speak infomally with sales and catering staff, when you are ready to ask for a written proposal on costs, most venues will expect you to present them with a Request For Proposal (or RFP), a written document that outlines what you expect from the facility and itemizes the services needed. This will help the staff at the venue prepare an accurate proposal for hosting your event.

Some venues make this easy by providing a form for you to fill out. For example, InterContinental Hotels Group has a link on its website at

www.meetings.ichotelsgroup.com where you can create and submit an RFP for any hotel in their chain simply by filling in the blanks.

International Association of Convention & Visitors Bureaus (IACVB) website has an online RFP form at **www.officialtravelinfo.com/meeting_planners.asp**. You can submit your request to convention and visitor bureaus (known as conference and/or tourism boards in many countries) in any of 500 destinations in 30 countries. Your RFP will be forwarded to local venues in those destinations, and they will provide you with proposals to host your event.

If you write your own RFP, remember to include these key elements:

- title and/or theme

- objective

- number of participants

- demographics of participants

- dates/number of days (including dates that are not available)

- food and beverage requirements

- number and size of meeting rooms

- number of sleeping rooms (total rooms multiplied by total nights)

- room set-up(s) and staging

- social functions planned, including off-property events

- support services needed

- range of rates sought

It's a good idea to speak to someone on site before you prepare your RFP. They may ask you questions that will help you prepare a more detailed and comprehensive document.

A sample RFP for hotel space for the Green World Forest Products Meeting could look like the one on the next page.

Sample Request For Proposal

ACME Event Management Ltd. Letterhead

To: (insert venue name and name of Sales Manager)

Green World Forest Products is a wood products manufacturer. We are planning a meeting of our sales staff in August 2004 to introduce new products to the sales teams and to reward high sales achievers. Our sales team is an energetic, casual and competitive group (75% male) ranging in age from 25-37.

I am seeking meeting and guestroom space for 35 participants, as follows:

Date: August 2004 – Any three-day weekday or weekend meeting agenda allowing a travel day at either end, except for the August 7 holiday weekend.

Rooms: Need rooms for 35 Green World participants and 2 ACME staff (30 single-occupancy rooms, 7 junior or executive suites). Rooms should be wired for Internet.

Meeting: One main meeting room to accommodate 35 participants, classroom style (two per table); one podium; data projector and screen; materials table at back of room and space for buffet table for mid-morning and early afternoon breaks.

Rate: $150.00-$170.00/night

Food and Beverage: Continental breakfast, two breaks, buffet lunch, pre-dinner host bar reception (all on a daily basis)

Please note: Participants will be transported off the grounds for dinner daily.

Please fax your response to my attention at 555-555-5555 by 4:00 p.m., Friday, March 19, 2004. If you cannot accommodate this event, please let me know so that I do not follow up with you.

Thank you,

Eva Eventplanner
ACME Event Management Ltd.

2.4.4 Site Inspection

One of the best ways for you to check out a venue in your area is to conduct a site inspection (or site survey). A site inspection is a visit to a venue to learn as much as possible about their facilities. You conduct a site inspection by calling ahead to arrange an appointment with the person who is in charge of renting the space or their representative. This could be the facility manager, events coordinator, or catering manager.

When you call to arrange the inspection make sure you get the contact's name, correct address and any driving instructions that may be needed. Tell them you are an event planner and would like to visit their facility when it is unoccupied and you are free to wander extensively.

Beware if the person on the phone tries to convince you not to visit and would rather just send you a brochure. Most reputable facilities will have marketing materials (brochures and such) on hand that they are more than happy to give you. However, the best opinion on what a facility is really like is yours. Have you ever booked a hotel room by simply seeing a brochure only to find out what looked like 1000 square feet turns out to be much smaller? A good photographer is like a magician and can make the smallest room seem like a palace.

Before you make your first appointment, design a simple site survey sheet that you can later refer to as a reminder of what you saw and, perhaps more importantly, didn't see. Include the name and address of the venue, the contact's name and phone number and an after hours contact name and number. On this sheet you can note the items listed above, plus any other observations – from the staff's attitude to the décor (or lack thereof). Your survey sheet could look something like the sample on the next page.

Add a large blank space for notes and comments. Your reputation as a professional is on the line here so take copious detailed notes. If you are not comfortable doing this during the site survey, take a few minutes to jot down your impressions as soon as you get in your car and before you drive to your next appointment. Typical comments could be: "great summer venue but not suitable for winter events"… "no handicapped facilities and difficult to get to"…."floors and carpets need to be replaced and walls are dingy"… etc.

Sample Site Survey Sheet

Venue:_____

Address:_____

Contact Name:_____ Title:_____

Phone Number:_____ Cell Phone:_____

Fax Number:_____ Email:_____

Website:_____

Seating capacity:_____

Number of rooms: _____

Floor plans available:_____

Parking spaces: Number: _____ Charge: _____

On Site Catering: _____

Staff:_____

Washrooms: Number: _____ Condition:_____

Handicapped facilities:

Washrooms:_____ Parking:_____ Ramps:_____

Deposit:_____

Cancellation policy:_____

Audiovisual capabilities:_____

Linens:_____

Table decorations:_____

Outdoor facilities:_____

Gratuities:_____

Janitorial service included:_____

Kitchen: Professional or Home style   Appliances:_____

Bar: Portable or Static: _____

Lighting: Natural:_____   Artificial:_____

Cleanliness:_____

2.4.5 Site Confirmation

Confirmation letters are less formal than a contract and provide the opportunity to clearly outline plans for the use of a facility or service. As with a contract, this letter allows an opportunity for any misunder-standings of expectations to be cleared up before the actual event. A confirmation letter should include:

- names of event planner and client

- dates of the event (include each day that the facility is required)

- detailed outline of space, services and equipment that will be provided

- any special considerations that have been established

- any payments (and deposits) that have already been made

- request for execution of signatures and return

A formal agreement will be entered into with the facility once the event planner's confirmation letter has been received and agreed to.

Sample Confirmation Letter

Mr. Marty Manager
Director of Sales
Sky High Hotel
22 Coastal Highway
Mega City, USA

Dear Mr. Manager,

Further to our telephone discussion and meeting of Monday, May 3, I would like to confirm that ACME Event Management, on behalf of its client, Windsor Widgets, intends to hold a one-day shareholders meeting at the Sky High Hotel. The particulars are as follows:

Event: Windsor Widgets Annual Shareholders Meeting

Date: Thursday, August 12, 2004

Space and Facility Requirements:

- 1 large meeting room to accommodate approximately 200 people seated theatre style, at a cost of $500.00

- 1 10' x 10' raised platform at front of room to hold 6' draped table

- 1 speaker stand (dais) equipped with microphone

- 1 projector and projection screen (screen to be placed behind the raised platform) at a rental cost of $125.00

- 1 registration desk area to accommodate a 10' draped banquet table, two chairs and telephone hookup. Installation and call charges to be charged to master account.

- 1 hospitality suite to be available between 7:00 a.m. and 6:30 p.m. on August 12, 2004, at a rate of $175.00

- 2 executive suite guestrooms for evening of August 11, 2004, at a rate of $275.00 per room per night.

Sky High Hotel acknowledges receipt of a deposit in the amount of $1,000.00 paid by Windsor Widgets, such amount to be deducted from the final invoice.

We look forward to working with you on the successful completion of our event. Please do not hesitate to call if you have any further questions or concerns.

Please sign this letter and return one copy to my attention at:

ACME Event Management Ltd.
555 Anywhere Street
Big City, USA

Regards,
Eva Eventplanner

We hereby agree with the contents contained herein and acknowledge receipt of this letter.

_____

Marty Manager,
Director of Sales, Sky High Hotel

Many facilities will have their own contract which they will want your client to sign to guarantee the booking. Make sure the contract is between the venue and your client, not between the venue and you. If you enter into a contract with a venue, you will be held personally liable for payment if the event is cancelled or postponed.

To help you ensure that everything is covered in your confirmation letter or contract, make a checklist for yourself of important points. Here is a sample venue checklist for a seminar, from the *FabJob.com Guide to Become a Motivational Speaker*.

Checklist to Discuss with Sales Coordinator

_____ Room set-up
_____ Start and end times (and if you need earlier access to room)
_____ Registration table (inside or outside room, number of chairs)
_____ Additional tables inside room for literature, displays, etc.
_____ Coat rack or coat check
_____ Audio-visual equipment (depending on your own needs)
     _____ microphone (clip-on is best for moving around)
     _____ overhead projector
     _____ flipchart or white board and markers
     _____ TV/VCR
     _____ sound system
     _____ plug-in for lap-top computer
_____ Stage or risers
_____ Notepads and pens or pencils for participants
_____ Coffee service
_____ Meals or snacks
_____ Delivery arrangements (if you need to ship supplies to hotel)
_____ Availability of parking for you and participants
_____ Access to public transportation
_____ Sleeping room for you (if out of town)
_____ Posting on hotel bulletin board (name of organization or title of event)
_____ Your phone number for people to call if they have inquiries

2.4.6 Pre-Event Meeting

Many event planners hold some type of Pre-Event or Pre-Conference meeting a couple of days before an event. It is simply a meeting of all of the individuals involved in the execution of the event to help ensure its success.

For a small event that does not include overnight stays, multiple meals and complicated travel arrangements the pre-event meeting might only involve the venue coordinator, caterer and the event planner. Plans for the event will be discussed ensuring everyone is on the right track and ready to go. Cellular telephone numbers and 24-hour emergency contact numbers may also be exchanged.

Event professionals planning large conferences or tradeshows that include hotel guest rooms, many catered events, countless travel arrangements, complicated space requirements, etc. will most certainly hold a pre-event meeting bringing together the major stakeholders of the event.   These meetings are usually held at the hotel/facility and could include:

- Meeting Professionals (you and your staff)

- Convention Service Manager

- Hotel Director of Sales

- Food & Beverage Manager, Catering/Banquet Manager and perhaps the Chef

- Hotel General Manager

- Representatives from these departments: Front Office, Reservations, Security, Housekeeping, Recreational Facilities, Telecommunication Services

It may seem like a lot of people and each hotel will have a different opinion on who and what departments need to be represented but one thing every facility agrees on is that you can not provide too much information about an event. The more information they have about the guests and the event the better.

2.5 Vendors

Many event planners are able to co-ordinate a number of events simultaneously while maintaining control over all the smallest details involved in each one. The question is: How do they manage?

Successful event planners have learned (sometimes the hard way) that they can't possibly attend to every detail of each event they are managing and now turn to the experts in the particular field for assistance. What this means is that event planners have become good "managers" and outsource or contract out many of the services they provide.

If you plan on working in-house for an event company, there may be staff already in place to assist with various tasks (e.g. printing). If you intend to become an independent event planner, you will want to assure your clients that you have the resources available to manage their event. The more services you can offer, the more value your client will perceive in hiring you. For this reason, it is imperative that you build a resource base of reliable vendors that you can outsource some tasks to in order to successfully complete an event.

Vendors (also known as "suppliers") are sellers of merchandise or services that may be used before, during or after an event. As an event planner, you will be working with many types of vendors. You will be expected to find and hire them (or recommend to your client which ones they should hire), as well as coordinate and supervise their work.

2.5.1 Types of Vendors

Following are some of the types of vendors that may be needed for an event. The list is not complete but will give you a good idea of how many different individuals and businesses are involved in the successful planning of an event.

- Audiovisual

- Balloons

- Caterers

- Equipment Rentals

- Florists

- Giftware

- Interpretation (for participants who speak a foreign language)

- Linens

- Mailing Houses

- Musicians

- Party Supply Rentals

- Photographers

- Printers

- Registration

- Security Companies

- Sign Shops

- Sound Systems

- Speakers (to speak at banquets and other events)

- Tent Rentals

- Transportation

- Travel Agents

Some of these services may be supplied by the venue you have booked. For example, if you are using a convention center they will supply tables and chairs, and you will likely be required to use their audiovisual supplier and catering services.

In other cases you may need many a wide variety of vendors in addition to those listed above. For example, if you are organizing a large outdoor event, you may need to find companies that rent bleachers, portable refrigerators, power generators, and portable sanitation units (toilets).

2.5.2 How to Find Vendors

For the new event planner, finding reliable suppliers can be a daunting task. Fortunately there are some great resources available to help you find vendors for just about any situation. For starters, check out two of the most popular magazines for the special events industry. Both of these magazines publish yearly source guides of vendors, and much of the information is available online.

Special Events Magazine publishes a Buyers Guide with dozens of categories covering virtually everything you might need for an event – from Access Doors to Wristbands. Although there is not a large selection of the usual types of vendors such as Photographers, this is a great place to find some of the not so usual, such as Dunking Machines, Robots, and Video Walls. Another excellent source of vendor information is published by *Event Solutions Magazine*.

- *Special Events Magazine Buyers Guide*
  http://specialevents.com/buyers_guide

- *Event Solutions Magazine National Source Book*
  www.event-solutions.com/articles/NatDir2003

- *Canadian Event Suppliers Guide* (coming in 2004)
  www.canadianspecialevents.com/cse/guide.html

Once you sign up on vendor mailing lists, you'll start receiving tons of useful information from suppliers, wholesalers and vendors. Start a good filing system so this information will be at your fingertips whenever you need it.

While websites and national directories can be excellent sources for vendors, don't neglect the local market. You'll want to consider going local on most services including catering, equipment rentals, and even entertainers (unless your budget allows for national acts).

In addition to the Yellow Pages and online searches, you may be able to find local suppliers through your Chamber of Commerce. Many chambers publish a membership directory which provides company contact information. You can also ask the venue you are working with for recommendations, as they are likely to know about a variety of local services.

2.5.3 Choosing Vendors

Before you can recommend vendors to your clients, you will need to check them out. One of the best ways for you to educate yourself about vendors in your area is to meet with them. Simply phone and ask to arrange an appointment with the owner or manager.

Solicit bids from at least two suppliers for each service. Compare prices, but pay careful attention to other "make or break" details. It is true that you often get what you pay for, so it's not always wise to go the cheapest route. Some key items to discuss before making your decision:

- price

- product specifications

- turnaround time

- delivery services

- customer service

- payment schedule

- deposits needed

Questions to Ask

To ensure you get all the information you need from your meeting, it's a good idea to come prepared with a list of specific questions to ask. You can either take notes on a notepad or design a "survey sheet" for each type of vendor you meet with. (A sample survey sheet for checking out a venue appears in section 2.4.4.)

The particular questions you use for a visit to a retailer, wholesaler or supplier will be tailored to the specific services they provide. For instance, you can ask a rental store if they deliver and set up. To illustrate, here are some questions you could ask a videographer, from the *FabJob.com Guide to Become a Wedding Planner*:

- How many hours will you work and what is the cost?

- Will you attend the rehearsal (what is the cost for this)?

- How much deposit is required and when is it payable?

- When is the final payment due?

- What is the cancellation policy?

- What are the overtime costs?

- How many cameras will be used?

- Will cordless microphones be used?

- Will the video be edited?

- Will any special effects be added (e.g. fading in or out)?

- Will music be added to the video?

- Does the package price include a certain number of videotapes?

- How much will it cost for additional videotapes?

- Are there any other costs?

- How long after the event will the video be available?

Finding Reputable Vendors

Perhaps the most important piece of advice we can give you about selecting vendors is to choose those who have a good reputation in the community and a great service record. As the event planner, your own reputation depends on the success or failure of vendor services. If possible, get referrals from people who have used them and had good luck. At the very least, ask potential suppliers for their letters of recommendation.

Before choosing a vendor, ask for references from previous clients. Call those references to find out what services the vendor provided, and whether the clients were satisfied. To uncover any problems, ask the client what they would do differently if they were hiring the same vendor, and which parts of the vendor's services they were least satisfied with. An article by Megan Rowe at **www.meetingsnet.com** offered a caution from Stephanie Downs, founder of ConferZone, about her experience with one supplier:

"Line up a supplier, but choose carefully. 'I was producing an event for a client and the company went bankrupt a week before the event,' says Downs, once a meeting planner herself... Ask questions about the firm's client base, how long it has been in business, whether it's profitable."

Even if all the references are positive, it's wise to contact your local Better Business Bureau to see if they have any complaints on file about the vendor. To locate a BBB anywhere in the U.S. or Canada visit their website at **www.bbb.org**.

Once you have planned a number of events you will know which vendors deliver what they promise and you will have built a preferred list of vendors you can recommend.

2.5.4 Vendor Contracts

Once you've selected your vendor, get it in writing! For some suppliers, a signed quote or spec sheet for the products you've chosen will suffice. In other cases, you could have a simple letter of understanding. (See the sample on the next page.)

For most vendors, however, a contract is critical. This is your insurance policy that the vendor will provide what you've agreed to. Most suppliers are familiar with and are comfortable working with contracts, and will probably be able to provide this document for you. Review it carefully before signing, and make sure all key points are covered. Some of the critical information that must be spelled out includes:

- Exactly what the vendor will (and will not) provide, e.g. if the vendor is a caterer and the venue is a community hall you need to know if the caterer will provide wait staff, linens, dishes, glasses, and set up/clean up staff.

- Exact times for set up, delivery, performance, etc.

- Any technical requirements or set up that you must provide.

- Detailed payment schedule, including deposits and when payment is due in full.

- Cancellation policy, including any fees payable if the event is cancelled.

Sample Initial Vendor Letter

ABC Bakery
123 Anywhere Road
Small Town, USA

Re: Jack Smith 50th Birthday Party – June 30, 2004

Dear Billy Baker,

I am writing you today to confirm the arrangements for the Smith birthday party, which is to take place June 30, 2004. As Event Planner for this party, I will be responsible for coordination of your services and will now be the contact person on any matters relating to the cake. My understanding of the arrangements is as follows:

- Birthday cake will be delivered to:
  The Central Park Hotel
  1131 Central Park Avenue
  Aspen Room (room layout attached)
- Cake to be delivered and set up by 3:30 p.m.
- Set up and decoration of cake table to be discussed

My client (Jill Smith) is responsible for payment to you for all services rendered including deposits and for any penalties or charges for cancellation of your service.

I will be sending a follow up letter to you two weeks before the party to ensure everything is in place and on schedule. Please feel free to contact me when/if the need arises. My contact information is as follows:

Eva Eventplanner
ACME Event Management
555 Anywhere Street
Big City, USA

Telephone: (888) 555-1212
Cellular: (888) 555-1234
Email: eva@evasevents.com

I look forward to working with your company again and I know Mr. Smith will be delighted with his cake.

Sincerely,
Eva Eventplanner
ACME Event Management

TIP: Some vendors will give you a "corporate rate" or subtract 10% from the price simply because you ask for a discount.

Remember, contracts are negotiable. If there is anything in the contract that you don't like, or anything you don't fully understand, discuss it before signing. Once that document is signed, you will have little recourse if something goes awry.

TIP: As mentioned under Venues, make sure the contract is between the vendor and your client, not between the vendor and you. If you enter into a contract with a vendor, you will be held personally liable for payment if the event is cancelled or postponed.

2.5.5 Tips for Specific Types of Vendors

The information above can help you work with virtually any type of vendor. The information in this section offers tips on working with some vendors that are frequently used by event planners. As mentioned above, several of these services may be provided by a single vendor such as the venue.

Travel and Transportation

If you've chosen a site for your event that is a considerable distance from your attendees' home base, you will have to arrange transportation to the venue. (Obviously this is not a necessary step for every function you organize, although many of today's thoughtful employers are providing transportation – via bus or taxi – to and from company events.)

There are four types of transportation needs you will encounter when planning events. The first three involve:

*   getting attendees to the host city via air, train, or bus

*   providing ground transportation to the hotel from the airport or train station

*   arranging group ground transporation for activities away from the hotel/venue

The fourth type of transportation needs involves arranging transportation for any goods required for the event, whether they're print and promotional materials or product samples. These materials will travel via cargo methods (such as forwarding agents) and may be subject to search if crossing international borders. It is wise to check with a customs or forwarding agent ahead of time when you are planning on shipping goods from one country to the next.

Air Travel

It is vital to have a transportation plan developed for the event. Once that is accomplished, a specialist (airline booking personnel or corporate travel agents) can be retained – usually at no additional cost – to find the lowest fares to the event, mail tickets, and handle individual traffic problems.

If you choose to use an airline specialist, they will usually provide complimentary or reduced rates for the event planner and their staff (i.e., one free ticket for every 50 sold). They may also offer negotiated air fare rates (a volume discount) and arrival and departure assistance specifically for your group.

If you end up planning a lot of conference or incentive travel, you would be wise to build a good relationship with a particular airline. Declare an airline to be the "official airline" of an event, or get discounts based on long-term exclusive use of one airline.

Usual lead times for booking travel arrangements are six to 12 months for a domestic location and eight to 18 months for an international location.

Ground Transportation

Ground transportation should be booked as far in advance as possible, taking into consideration other events that may be happening in that locale. Try to get a signed contract at least six months in advance. It is also advisable to get at least three proposals. Here are some important questions to ask ground transportation providers:

- What condition and age is the company's fleet of vehicles?

- What is the capacity of the vehicles?

- Are they accessible to people with disabilities?

- Are the vehicles insured with one million dollars of liability insurance?

- Are the vehicles air-conditioned and do they provide restroom facilities?

- Does the driver provide assistance with storing luggage?

- What type of contingency plans does the supplier have?

- Does the supplier have enough vehicles to handle the entire group?

If you are booking taxis or limo services for a local function most of the questions above will still apply (except for restroom facilities).

Food and Beverage Service

In spite of impeccable planning and an otherwise fabulous event, your efforts can be negated by poor quality food and service. The best way to prevent this from happening is to plan a menu that is balanced nutritionally and appeals to many differing tastes — and use suppliers who are proven to provide great food and friendly service.

Special food needs can easily be met by canvassing your attendees for dietary concerns (kosher, vegetarian, gluten free, etc.) and, in turn, passing those on to the caterer for consideration.

When planning meals for conferences, event planners have learned it is good practice to provide a somewhat substantial mid-morning break for those participants who do not eat breakfast first thing in the morning or for those who prefer to sleep in a little later.

Don't try to reduce food costs by eliminating mid-morning and afternoon breaks. Not only do they provide needed restroom breaks, but offering a bit of refreshment will also help to re-energize people after sitting for long periods of time. Get creative with these breaks — instead of providing cookies and squares, try an ice-cream bar or popcorn vending machine. If at all possible, these breaks should also take place outside of the meeting room.

Experienced planners and clients who sponsor many of these events also know it is wise not to provide a long break for lunch. Attendees will be tempted to leave the building and the first session after lunch may be quite chaotic due to this.

In addition to conferring with the site's event coordinator, you might also meet with the venue's wine steward and catering manager to assist in planning any food service requirements. Trust these people's judgment on items and allow them to assist in choosing appropriate wine and food pairings.

Entertainers and Speakers

For some events – such as a fundraiser featuring a celebrity – an entertainer or speaker is the focus of an event. At other events, entertainers may simply be a nice touch. There are a variety of types of entertainers you can hire for an event, including:

- Caricature Artists
- Celebrities (either to speak or simply sign autographs)
- Celebrity Impersonators
- Clowns
- Comedians
- Dancers
- Emcees
- Hypnotists
- Jugglers
- Magicians
- Singers
- Speakers

You may find entertainers and speakers through word of mouth, the Internet, or even the Yellow Pages. However, most professional entertainers are represented by agencies, while professional speakers are represented by speakers bureaus. Agencies and bureaus have usually pre-screened all the acts they represent. However, before hiring an entertainer or speaker, make sure you ask for references and view their demo tape to ensure they are right for your group.

An excellent place to find vendors online is the PartyPop.com vendor directory. They have links to entertainers from A (Acrobats) to V (Ventriloquists) at **www.partypop.com/Categories/Entertainment.html**.

You can find local speakers by checking the Yellow Pages under "speakers". To find nationally known speakers, contact a speakers bureau such as Speakers Platform at 877-717-LEARN (5327) or **www.speaking.com**. You can also find bureaus listed by country, state, and city at **www.findspeakersandbureaus.com** (you'll need to complete a free registration process to access the information).

Bureaus can save you time by recommending only those speakers that are appropriate for your event. Even better, there is no charge for their services, because bureaus are paid by the speakers. However, most bureaus will only represent speakers that charge at least $1,000 per presentation, so if your budget is limited you will have to track down a speaker without a bureau's help.

Working with VIPs

If your event includes VIPs such as celebrities or visiting dignitaries, you'll need to make some special efforts to ensure that these guests are treated well. *Meeting Planners Handbook 2002* offers a number of good tips, including:

- Designate a reliable individual as liaison

- Arrange for a gift basket in the hotel room

- Make special arrangements so the VIP doesn't have to stand in the registration and/or buffet line

- Review seating, introduction and receiving line protocol, if applicable.

- Double-check the spelling of the VIP's name, title, company or rank for accuracy on all written material

Contacting Celebrities

If you are willing to pay celebrities to appear at your event (expect to spend thousands of dollars for an appearance fee plus travel expenses), you can use a speakers bureau to arrange the booking. Virtually all bureaus know how to track down any celebrity.

If you are hoping to get a celebrity to make a donation of their services, an item to be auctioned, etc., you will need to contact them directly. Celebrities can be contacted through the organizations they work with (for example, famous authors can be found through their publishers). However, you'll have better results if you track down a celebrity through their official website or agent.

Celebrity Addresses Online charges a small fee ($6.95 for a three day trial or $19.95 for a printed directory) and guarantees accurate contact information for more than 15,000 celebrities. They have contact information for movie, TV, music, and sports stars (including their agent, manager, publicist, production companies, record company, etc.) as well as politicians, models, authors, directors, artists, world leaders, fashion designers, Nobel Prize Winners, and many other public figures. Visit **www.celebrity-addresses.com**.

Photographers

No matter what type of event you are planning, having a photographer record the highlights is a nice touch. It is also practical as well. If the event is a recurring one, it will be easier to entice previous attendees to return by reminding them through pictures of how much fun the event was. Photos from earlier events provide great material for promoting future events on websites and in newspapers, magazines and posters.

Use the same criteria when hiring a photographer as you would with any other supplier. Ask to see examples of previous work and ask for references. A top photographer should be booked at least 10 months in advance, or more, if the event takes place during wedding season.

Be sure to specify in the contract exactly how long the photographer will be at the event and how many rolls of film will be shot for the agreed-upon price.

Clearly outline the type of photos you are after (beautiful venue shots, people only, or a mix) and advise the photographer that some of the shots will be used for future promotions.

> **TIP:**   You can also add these photos to your personal portfolio to promote yourself.

Audiovisual Requirements

Once you know who your entertainers and speakers are, you can contact them to find out what audio/visual needs they have. For example, most speakers use some form of visual aid when delivering their speech and some will want their presentation taped.

Many venues offer some A/V service, either in-house or through an affiliated company. Make sure you understand exactly what is available, and compare it with your requirements. Be sure to consider what kind of hi-tech equipment you may need, including Internet access.

Some venues require you to work with their own companies, while others will allow you to bring in your own equipment or hire an outside company to handle it. You'll want to discuss this in advance to avoid any unpleasant surprises.

Make sure you have good technical support planned for the day of the event. We've all been to meetings where the moderator couldn't get the VCR to work, or the Power-Point display went blank due to a computer malfunction. Plan a technical run-through to test the setup and function of all equipment as part of your dress rehearsal to avoid any embarrassment.

Printers

Almost every event will require some form of print products, from programs, signs, nametags, poster-sized agendas, day-at-a-glance agendas to promotional materials and handouts. The requirements for the event you are planning are dictated by the event itself. For instance, are there multi-day activities? If so, personal day-at-a-glance agendas (or daily event agendas) are a nice touch for attendees. Does the event require attendees to use a ticket to gain entry?

Each element of a printing process will have an estimated deadline. Work with your chosen printer to determine the deadlines. A rough estimate is 1 to 8 weeks if the process runs smoothly. Discuss delivery schedules well in advance, and allow a good month for design and printing of materials if possible. Build this time into your planning schedule to avoid last-minute mailings and missed deadlines.

Most printers can also recommend good graphic designers, and some even have them in-house. This is a great option, especially if you're pressed for time, but always ask for and receive a written quote on all printed pieces.

Designing Invitations Yourself

Some event planners enjoy designing the invitations and other printed materials themselves. Doing so allows you the opportunity to show off your creative side and will also be cheaper than hiring a designer. Once the initial software package has been paid for you will be able to use it over and over again and updates to the package should be free.

Software such as Microsoft's Greetings package at **www. home-greetings.com** turns out Hallmark quality greetings, invitations, banners etc. in minutes. There are many more choices of software available. Check with your favorite software supplier or office supplies store or ask around to see what other professionals are using. If you do decide to design and print your own invitations, and perhaps smaller items like name tags, keep in mind that your printed goods should have a consistent look, feel and color.

2.5.6 Coordination with the Suppliers

Prior to the event, ask for one contact at each supplier and touch base with them. Sometimes it's helpful to hold a vendor meeting, especially when planning a large event, in order to discuss delivery logistics and any possible interference or conflicts. It just won't do to have your caterer's truck blocked by the sound van in the delivery bay, so coordinating the schedule is a must!

Make sure all vendors have your cell phone and office numbers, and enter their numbers into your phone book for easy reference.

2.6 Marketing

Effective marketing is critical to the success of any event. It ensures that the event is well attended and that the event's objectives are achieved.

For many events, marketing is handled by an individual or group that specializes in marketing, public relations or advertising. A non-profit organization may have a public relations committee, while a corporation will have a department or at least a coordinator on staff. Large organizations may also retain a public relations firm or advertising agency. In any of these situations, you will act as a liaison with the marketing people, and assist in coordinating any logistics.

With other events, you may be expected to oversee marketing yourself as part of your event planning services.

Whether you are doing it yourself, or working with marketing people, the first step will be to develop a marketing plan. This will be part of the timeline schedule and critical path described earlier. Brainstorm ideas for advertising and promoting the event. If the event has been held before, your client can tell you how it was promoted in the past, and how effective those marketing techniques were.

Chances are you will come up with more ideas than time and money will allow you to implement. So decide with the client which marketing techniques will be used for the event, based on the available financial and human resources. For example, the items on your list might include:

- Direct mail

- Brochures

- Posters

- Billboards

- Newspaper advertising

- Radio advertising

- Contacting media with ideas for feature stories

- Event calendar listings

- Cable TV spots

- Invite the media to the event

- Develop a media kit to distribute at the event

You will then need to break down each marketing technique into specific steps, with deadlines, and someone responsible for ensuring it gets done. For example, if you are planning to advertise, you will need to arrange to have the ad designed, have the design approved by the client, get any revisions to the ad, book the space or time in the appropriate media outlets, submit the ad by the deadline, and arrange for payment.

2.6.1 Advertising

Media Advertising

Advertising includes paid placement in newspapers, magazines, journals, television, radio and online media, where you pay for the spot and control the entire message. Use ads to boost registrations and ticket sales and as a way to highlight sponsors.

However, advertising is extremely expensive. Even a tiny ad (2 inches square) in a major metropolitan newspaper can cost hundreds of dollars. Television advertising runs to thousands of dollars, and radio advertising is often ineffective unless numerous spots are purchased.

As an alternative to buying advertising at full prices, contact local media outlets to see if they will be a "media sponsor" for the event. A media sponsor donates a number of free ads in return for getting recognition in other media where the event is being advertised, as well as on event printed materials (e.g. tickets, banners, programs, etc.) You will need to contact the media outlet's promotions department as far in advance of the event as possible, and they may require that the client pay for some of the advertising.

Use your negotiating skills (see the next chapter) and explain to the media outlet the benefits of getting involved with your particular event. For example, if you are pitching the event to a newspaper, you might explain how they will reach prospective readers and advertisers, as well as being associated with a popular community event.

If you do not have media sponsorship, consider trying small classified or display ads in your local newspaper or a newsletter read by your intended audience. Your ad should include a large heading that promises a benefit. In addition to at least one benefit, your ad should include the event date, time, cost, and where to get more information. Here's an example for a publishing conference:

PUBLISH YOUR BOOK
Find out how you can become a published author at a conference on Saturday January 30 from 10 am to 4 pm at the Civic Center. Tickets are almost sold out, so register early. Call Conferences Unlimited at 555-1212 or visit www.pubconf.com.

Direct Mail

Most organizations have a mailing list, and systems in place for sending mail to the people on their list. If the organization wants to try mailing invitations or promotional brochures to new prospects, they will need to rent a mailing list.

One way to get a list is to contact associations or magazine publishers to see if they are willing to rent their list to promote the event. Online, search for "mailing lists" or "mailing list broker" (a broker can give you advice about the best lists to choose) or check the Yellow Pages under "mailing lists." Brokers and companies that sell lists can help you find lists broken down by geographic area, number of employees, industry, etc.

Buying a list from a broker typically costs about 5 to 25 cents per name. With the cost of brochure and postage on top of that, you can expect to spend about $1 per mailing. Before doing a large mailing you should test a list by mailing to a small group first. You can find helpful advice on using direct mail through the U.S. Postal Service at **www.usps.com/directmail/dmguide** and **www.usps.com/businessmail101**.

Brochures

When preparing brochures, focus on communicating all the benefits of attending. Benefits of attending an event may include:

- a fun night out
- supporting a good cause
- reconnecting with old friends
- learning something new
- networking
- hearing a celebrity speak (or meeting a celebrity)
- keeping up with current trends in the industry

Among the other items you might include in a brochure:

- Who should attend

- When and where the event takes place

- Information about the entertainers or speakers

- Testimonials (e.g. from someone who attended last year)

- That seats are limited (mention if past events sold out)

- A call to action such as "Get your tickets now!"

- How to register, including your phone number and web site

The ideal brochure for a public event is one that can double as a poster (e.g. printed on one side of a colorful 8½" x 11" sheet). Post them on public bulletin boards and, if permitted, boards at bookstores and college campuses.

2.6.2 Publicity

Publicity Before the Event

The best way to market an event – with the greatest number of attendees for the lowest cost – is to get free media publicity before the event. While you don't have the final say over what gets reported, the exposure can give a tremendous boost to ticket sales.

To market your event, submit a summary of your event details (date, time, theme, cost, what's happening, etc.) to any upcoming events columns in local newspapers and magazines. If your client is a non-profit organization, type "Public Service Announcement" at the top of the notice, and send it to radio stations and cable TV stations as well.

If you have a celebrity, speaker, or an articulate entertainer who will be appearing at the event, contact local media to arrange interviews before the event. Long distance telephone interviews can be done by local newspapers and radio stations. Newspapers can do interviews by email as well.

Radio Interviews

For radio, contact talk show producers, news directors, or morning show hosts, depending on who you think would be most interested in your topic. When you contact them, be sure to emphasize how much the show's audience will benefit from an interview. Keep in mind that they are not interested in giving you free advertising – their ultimate goal is to improve their ratings, so anyone they interview should be dynamic and interesting.

Also, keep in mind that many station employees are overworked and underpaid. If you can make their job easier you are much more likely to land an interview. The best way to make their job easier is to include a list of "frequently asked questions" with the letter or news release you send them. This is a list of questions that you think listeners might like the answers to. For example, to promote a Singles Conference, you can include questions such as "What are the best places to meet people?"

Newspaper and Magazine Publicity

One way to get a story written about your upcoming event is to send a press release (also called a "news release") to a writer, magazine editor, or the editor of the appropriate section of the newspaper. Depending on the event, that may be the Entertainment, Business, Lifestyle, or another part of the paper. (If the editor's name is not published in the paper, you can call and ask the receptionist.)

Your press release should be written so that it could be published "as is." Read the magazine or section of the paper where you would like to be published and use a similar writing style for your own news release. Remember, it should read like a news story, not an advertisement. Here are some other tips for writing a press release.

- Make sure the press release is newsworthy. A large community festival is newsworthy. A business meeting is not, unless something unusual is on the agenda or someone interesting will be speaking.

- Give your press release a strong lead paragraph that answers the six main questions: who, what, where, when, why, and how.

- Keep it short. Aim for a maximum of 500 words.

- Include contact information at the end of the press release so that reporters and readers can get tickets.

Sample News Release

Thelma Therapist
ABC Massage Therapy
123 Health Lane
Anytown, USA 12345
(xxx)xxx-xxxx
therapy@email.com

For Immediate Release
January xx, 200x

Free Workshop on *The Power of Touch*

A free workshop demonstrating the power of touch will be given at the Anytown USA Chamber of Commerce, located at 1234 Business Road, on January xx, 20xx from 7pm to 9pm.

Thelma Therapist will share results from a number of research studies involving massage therapy, including premature babies, the elderly, colic, diabetes, depression, and sleep disturbances. The latest research proves the efficacy of massage.

Ms. Therapist, in practice since 200x, will talk about the positive effects massage can have on pain and illness, as well as an overall wellness tool for everyday life. She graduated from The Massage Institute in Anytown, USA.

For more information, call the Anytown USA Chamber of Commerce at (xxx)xxx-xxxx.

###

This sample news release is adapted from the *FabJob.com Guide to Become a Massage Therapist*, by Sharon A. Alfonso, LMT. For additional tips on writing news releases visit **www.publicityinsider.com/release.asp**.

Invite the Media to the Event

To get media to cover the event, contact the assignment editor at TV stations, the news director at radio stations, and the appropriate editors at magazines and newspapers. Remember to include any "society" columns which might run a photo of the organization executive members and guest speaker.

A good way to invite the media is by sending a media advisory. This is a one page document which you can fax, email or mail. The following template for a media advisory is provided by Real World PR at **www. realworldpr.com**.

Sample Media Advisory Format

For Immediate Release

* * * MEDIA ALERT * * *
* * * PHOTO OPPORTUNITY * * *

[Headline Goes Here, Initial Capped, Bold and Centered]

WHAT: [A brief description of the event goes here]

WHO: [Key players in event]

WHEN: [Date, day of week, and start and end times of event]

WHERE: [location and address and site location go here]

BACKGROUND: [Additional background about event goes here (if necessary) or company boilerplate (a brief description of the company, and any information you want readers to know about it, such as what type of business it is in, what its annual sales are, where it is headquartered, where branch offices are located, the number of employees, etc.)]

# # #

For more information, contact:
[contact information goes here]

Make sure you are prepared to work with any media that attend the event. You should have: a volunteer or staff member to assist them, someone they can interview, and media kits.

A media kit is a two-pocket folder (either purchased from a stationery store, or printed with your client's logo) with information about the event and the organization. Your media kit might include:

- News release

- Fact sheet

- Backgrounder

- Brochure

- Biography of the CEO or celebrity speaker

- Photographs

- Photocopies of news stories about past events

- Small promotional items (e.g. bookmark, postcard, etc.)

You can find templates to help you create items for your media kit at **www.aboutpr.com/subpages/samples/press_release_format.htm**.

2.6.3 Sponsorships

If your client is an association or non-profit organization, chances are they will want to find sponsors to cover some or all of the costs of putting on the event. There are several different ways that sponsors can make a contribution to an event:

- Donate money

- Donate an item for a door prize, raffle, or silent auction

- Donate services or products required to put on the event (for example, a printer could donate all the printing for the event)

- Donate items to include in gift bags for attendees

EXAMPLE: An article titled "Gift Bags: You Can Take It With You" in *Special Events Magazine* (June, 2003), reported that "More than 500 gift bags — each valued at about $3,500 — tempted Sundance film festival party guests with such treats as Nautica ski gear and one-year membership passes to hip Crunch Fitness gyms."

Where the Money Is

Don't limit your search for potential sponsors to head offices of major corporations. Many small companies and regional offices will sponsor local events.

Start by asking your client for lists of previous sponsors, current members or volunteers who own a company, and any personal connections your client or committee has with companies that might sponsor the event.

If you are seeking a donation of services from a small company, the ideal person to speak with is the company owner. With large companies, most people seeking donations usually apply to the Public Relations Department, the Marketing Department, or the President.

Public Relations Department

Sometimes known as "Corporate Communications," these departments often have control over a company's donations to the community. This department typically provides funding for groups involved with education, the arts, health care and community organizations such as United Way.

One Corporate Donations Coordinator said she hears every day from individuals and organizations seeking funding. She reviews each proposal to see if it fits within the company's funding guidelines (see the TIP on the next page). Those that fit the guidelines are forwarded to a donations committee that meets several times per year. The donations committee chooses the causes they feel are most deserving and successful applicants receive checks. Fewer than 5% of applications are successful, and an applicant might wait several months to hear they have been turned down.

TIP: Before applying for financial support to a Public Relations or Corporate Communications department, phone or email and ask for the donations guidelines. If they do not specifically state that they fund events such as the one you are planning, contact the company's Marketing Department or President instead.

Marketing Department

In many companies Marketing is the department that is most likely to sponsor community events. When approaching the Marketing Department, it is important to keep in mind that unlike the Public Relations Department, which makes donations to 'good causes,' this department is focused on what the company will get in return for their sponsorship.

Trying to convince them how much you 'need' money is a waste of energy. Thousands of events need money. This department wants to know that if they invest in your event, they will see a return on investment (ROI).

Exactly what they want will vary from one company to another, but most companies want to enhance their image, increase awareness of their brand, gain visibility for their products and increase sales. By sponsoring an event, a company can achieve these goals through association with a high profile event and:

- having their company logo, name or advertisement seen by people attending the event (on tickets, banners, programs, posters, ads for the event, etc.)

- having their logo potentially seen by thousands of other people through the event's media coverage (for example, if their logo is on a banner or podium that appears in a television story about the event).

To find out what a particular company wants, call the Marketing Department and ask to meet with them to discuss how the company might benefit by sponsoring you.

Sample Letter Seeking a Donation

Sunnyday Humane Society

September 6, 2003

Attention: Jane Jeweler
Jane's Jewelry Store
FAX: 555-1212

Dear Jane:

I am writing to ask if Jane's Jewelry would contribute to a raffle we are holding as part of a special event at Mega Mall.

The event is called "For the Love of Animals" and will take place at Mega Mall in downtown Sunnyday on Saturday, November 8. We anticipate a tremendous turn-out for this fun-filled day which will feature media personalities, displays, and some of our animals awaiting adoption.

The Sunnyday Humane Society has a strong community base of 10,000 members and donors, many of whom we believe will come to Mega Mall for the day to show their support. We are expecting this to be a well publicized event with plenty of media coverage. As a donor, we would ensure that your store is acknowledged in our signage and promotional literature.

Donations allow us to keep our doors and our hearts open. We are grateful for a donation of any size.

Please call me at 555-1234 when you have an opportunity to consider what your company would be comfortable contributing. We are grateful for any support you can give us and hope you will be participating in "For the Love of Animals".

Yours sincerely,

Eva Eventplanner

TIP: A personal meeting with a decision-maker is MUCH more likely to result in a donation than simply mailing a written proposal. If you are asked to submit something in writing, ask to arrange a meeting so you can discuss it in person.

The President's Office

In some companies, especially smaller ones, the President or Chief Executive Officer can decide on their own to sponsor your event. In these cases, you don't need to make a formal written proposal or jump through hoops. Instead, the President may decide to have the company sponsor you based on a personal meeting.

Even if the company has formal sponsorship procedures in place, having this person's support can make it faster and easier for you to get sponsorship. The President can put you in touch with the right people in the organization, give a personal recommendation and help cut through any corporate red tape. If someone on your committee knows the President, it's ideal to have them call, or to mention that person's name when you call.

TIP: Phoning to ask for donations is often more effective than writing. The information in the sample letter on the facing page can be communicated in a telephone call as well.

More information about sponsorships is available through IEG at **www.sponsorship.com/sponsor**.

2.7 Event Day

It's finally here! The big day! After all the planning, prodding and producing, you're probably feeling a range of emotions from excitement to nervousness to sheer terror. Use those feelings to keep your energy up (you're going to need every ounce of it today!) but don't give into the jitters.

To ensure the day goes as smoothly as possible, make sure that everyone with a key role is given an event itinerary so they know where they should be and what they should be doing throughout the day. A sample itinerary is shown on the next page.

Sample Event Day Itinerary

Groundbreaking Event
April 20, 2004
Itinerary

7:00 a.m.   Charter plane leaves Denver
                     Acme Aviation, 234 Aviation Avenue

7:57 a.m.   Arrival in Rockytown
                     Our group will be picked up at airport and taken to
                     XYZ Building

9:00 a.m.   Management Committee Meeting
                     Boardroom (Room 200), XYZ Building

10:00 a.m.   Meeting of support staff who will be coordinating
                     groundbreaking
                     Room 100, XYZ Building

11:00 a.m.   Meeting of groundbreaking event speakers
                     Boardroom (Room 200), XYZ Building

11:15 a.m.   This is the time groundbreaking guests have been
                     invited to arrive

11:30 a.m.   Groundbreaking ceremony at Construction site

12:00 p.m.   Luncheon guests begin to arrive at the Civic Centre
                     555 Civic Street, Rockytown
                     A bus will be available to drive you to the luncheon

12:15 p.m.   Buffet service begins

2:30 p.m.   Bus or van service from Civic Centre to the airport

3:00 p.m.   Charter flight leaves Rockytown

4:09 p.m.   Arrive in Denver

Here are some other tips to make event day a success:

- Arm your volunteers, workers and suppliers with telecommunications equipment (such as 2-way radios and cell phones) to enable them to have easy access to you, each other and emergency contacts.

- Wear comfortable shoes and clothing that won't restrict your movement.

- Keep your program binder (or whatever holds your paperwork) with you at all times. This is the blueprint for the entire event and will tell you where everyone should be at any given moment and what they should be doing.

- Remember that even seasoned event planners have the unexpected happen. Designate someone (such as your assistant) to be your backup. Make sure she knows what should be happening during the event, and has copies of important papers from your program binder. If you are pulled away to deal with something, she should be able to jump in and take over for you.

- Prepare an emergency kit that includes pens, paper, tape, extra name tags, contact numbers, aspirin, extra keys to facilities or storage areas, a couple of energy bars and bottled water.

- Try to maintain control of your emotions at all times. In an April 2003 article at Meetings and Conventions Online, Louise M. Flesher says: "Keep breakdowns private. Never let them see you cry. Just as you have mapped out emergency routes for attendees, find emergency meltdown stations — your hotel room, a stall in an empty bathroom, behind a large ficus plant. Knowing you have a secret hideout for a brief implosion can be a natural Prozac that prevents an emotional overload."

2.8 After the Event

You've made it! The last balloon has popped, the last door prize has been given away, and you've pulled off a successful, well-organized event. Sit back and relax, but don't get too comfy — you've still got some work to do! In this section, we'll give you some hints to help you wrap up the loose ends neatly and lay the groundwork for next year's success.

2.8.1 Event Evaluations

Appraising the success of the event can be accomplished through program evaluation and feedback from attendees, sponsors, exhibitors and suppliers. The evaluation may be tailored to rate one aspect of an event (such as a speaker) or it could be a more all-encompassing one including questions on the total experience. Samples of both appear on the next few pages.

Wise event planners know to include time for evaluations into the agenda close to the end of the event to elicit feedback on the program. If this is not possible, evaluations could also be mailed out post-event to those who attended. Mail-out evaluations are not as effective, and the number of responders will drop significantly. To entice attendees to fill out an evaluation, you could have a drawing for prizes for those who respond.

It will be difficult to get written feedback at festivals (particularly those held outdoors), weddings and other family gatherings. However, you could canvass a cross-section of people attending an outdoor event and entice them with giveaways or prizes if they respond to your evaluation before leaving.

The information gathered from evaluations can be used to plan future events (e.g. choosing suppliers, speakers, venues), to measure whether stated goals were met, and to make recommendations to clients.

Use these guidelines when creating your evaluation forms:

- Ask specific questions. For instance, don't ask, "How would you rate the meals, facilities and guestrooms?" These items should be rated separately.

- Make it easy to respond. Evaluations should be confidential (don't ask for names), short and concise, with easy-to-follow directions.

- Make collections convenient. Receptacles should be clearly marked and placed in a convenient location (e.g. at meeting room exits).

Sample Conference Evaluation

Please take a few minutes to provide your comments on the conference by completing this form and placing it in the receptacle provided at the exits. Your input is valuable and will assist us in improving future events. Thank you!

Based on the content and delivery, please rate the speakers:

Speaker:	Poor		Average		Excellent
John Smith	1	2	3	4	5
Susan Simmons	1	2	3	4	5
Alicia Wong	1	2	3	4	5

Based on your experience at this conference, please rate the following:

Activity:	Poor		Average		Excellent
On-site registration	1	2	3	4	5
Conference facilities	1	2	3	4	5
Food and beverage	1	2	3	4	5
Contents and topics	1	2	3	4	5
Agenda	1	2	3	4	5
Cost/value	1	2	3	4	5
Off-site activities	1	2	3	4	5

To help us identify possible areas for improvement, please answer the following questions:

1. What did you like best about the conference? Least?

2. How can we improve the conference?

3. Which topics would you like to see included in future events?

4. Do you have any final comments or suggestions?

May we use your comments in future promotional materials?
Yes ___ No ___

Name: _____ Company: _____

If you would like to be contacted regarding your comments, please provide the following information:
Phone: _____ Email: _____

Sample Speaker Evaluation

Speaker's Name: _____

Title of Presentation: _____

1. How would you rate this presentation's content?

Excellent ___ Very Good ___ Average ___ Acceptable ___ Poor ___

2. How closely did the program content correspond to your needs and interests?

Excellent ___ Very Good ___ Average ___ Acceptable ___ Poor ___

3. Rate the following aspects of the speaker's presentation:

	Poor		**Average**		**Excellent**
Overall Performance	1	2	3	4	5
Knowledge of Topics	1	2	3	4	5
Ability to Answer Questions	1	2	3	4	5

General Comments:

1. What did you find most useful about this program?

2. How could this program be improved?

3. Other comments

Feel free to bask in the applause, but listen carefully to the negative comments. These are the keys to becoming a better event planner, so take them seriously. Of course, there will always be a curmudgeon or two in the crowd, but if several guests complain about a particular aspect, you know you have something that should be changed for the next event.

If someone makes a legitimate complaint, take the time to thank them for their input. While this can be hard to do, it is important for the guests to know their complaints will be taken seriously.

Evaluating Marketing Results

Advertising and publicity should have a measurable effect on your event. For example, an ad designed to sell advance tickets will, hopefully, result in increased ticket sales. In order to gauge the results of your media placements, build in some sort of tracking system.

For example, staff can keep a simple tally when taking calls for an event. Brochures and mailings are easy to track, but use a photocopy of the actual form when taking ticket orders in house. This will help you track the results of your direct marketing efforts and distinguish mail-ins from phone-ins.

2.8.2 Other Activities

Financial Matters

Now that the event is over and actual expenses are in you can reconcile the budget to actual expenses. Just as you would carefully check your personal power bill before paying you will scrutinize the invoices from all suppliers before approving for payment.

Post-Event Meeting

A post-event meeting follows the conclusion of the event and the same people who attended the pre-event meeting should be included. The reason for this meeting is to collect impressions on how the event was handled and to learn ways to correct shortcomings or to make the next conference better. This is not a time to assign blame to any one department or person if something went wrong.

Mistakes do happen, and while it's all too easy to assign blame, get the facts before you act. For instance, if the ground transportation company goes to the wrong pick-up spot, yelling at the driver is not going to help matters any. You will look unprofessional and, in fact, it may not be the driver's fault. You or your assistant may have transposed a number when typing the address.

Calmly and professionally take up the matter with the manager or owner at a meeting or during a phone call set up for this purpose. Work with the management to find a solution for future events and send a follow-up letter outlining your understanding of the events and the steps to take to avoid a future mistake.

Thank Yous and Acknowledgements

If you've made it to the end of the event, and you're still standing and smiling, you have a lot of people to thank! VIPs, speakers, sponsors, committee members, staff, volunteers — there are undoubtedly many, many people who deserve a pat on the back for helping you pull it off. Whatever you choose – thank you letters, handwritten notes, gift baskets, flowers, etc. – make it personal and sincere.

One word of caution. The thank you letter is not the place to note problems or complaints. Save that for the wrap-up meeting!

Planning For Next Year

If this is an annual event, now is great time to lay the groundwork for next year. The earlier you book your event and begin planning, the easier your work becomes.

If you loved working with a particular vendor, note that in your file. Conversely, flag any problem vendors. Book a date for next year, and get tentative commitments from sponsors. Solicit more volunteer help, and keep staff involved and motivated. Play off the current excitement to get buy-in for next year!

3. Preparing for Your Career

By now you've realized that an event planner has to manage a huge number of details at once and keep all the balls in the air, appear calm under fire, and be the ultimate host or hostess. This takes some special skills, including attention to detail, follow-through, and good organizational traits. It also helps if you can handle the unexpected and change directions quickly, and have a knack for dealing with people.

In this chapter we will outline the skills you need to succeed in your new fab job, and give you some terrific resources to help you acquire and hone these skills.

3.1 Skills

What does it take to be a success in this field? Let's take a closer look at some of the traits and skills you'll need.

3.1.1 Interpersonal Skills

Events are about people, whether they're guests, attendees, clients, or vendors. Here are some key interpersonal skills and why they can be so helpful to your career:

Relationship Building

Building good relationships is important to the success of any event. Ideally, everyone involved with the event, from the ticket takers to the florist to the VIPs, will walk away feeling great about the experience. To do this, you will have to ensure that everyone gets what they need out of the experience, and talking to them is the only sure fire way to learn this. Be friendly, be sincere, engage in small talk and learn more about the person you're dealing with.

These behaviors can help not only during an event – they can help you get hired. If you are like most of us, one of the reasons you continue to do business with certain people is because you like them.

When it comes to hiring an event planner, employers and clients usually have a number of event planners to choose from. Given a choice between two capable people, the job will often go to the person who is well-liked. In fact, when people like you, their feelings toward you can extend to their perception of your work (this is called "the halo effect"). So they may actually see your work in a more positive light because they like you.

In addition to developing relationships with clients, event planners also need to develop relationships with vendors. Having a good relation-ship with vendors can help you get what you want when you need something in a rush or when you need something that's difficult to track down. A supplier who likes you will be more likely to go the extra mile for you, which in turn will help you look good to your client.

Traits that can help you build good relationships are a positive attitude and enthusiasm. Nothing builds excitement about an event faster than a planner who is passionate about the affair. If you project a positive, enthusiastic attitude, others will naturally be drawn to you and want to be involved.

Be upfront and honest about challenges and obstacles when appro-priate, but never complain about how much work you have to do or how hard a particular task is to complete. Remain upbeat and high-charged, and you'll generate a real buzz about your event. And per-haps most importantly – do whatever it takes to keep your word.

An excellent resource to build stronger relationships is the classic book *How to Win Friends and Influence People*, by Dale Carnegie.

Communication Skills

Verbal Skills

Verbal communication skills come into play when you are selling your-self to potential clients. If you are dealing with corporate clients, chances are they are articulate and professional, and are likely to be comfort-able hiring an event planner who "speaks their language."

To improve your verbal communication skills, ask friends or a vocal coach for feedback on any areas that could be improved, such as: use of slang, proper grammar, or altering your tone of voice to eliminate any harshness. (You can find vocal coaches in the Yellow Pages.)

Listening

Being a good listener can help ensure you come up with something that the client wants. While listening seems like an easy skill to master, most of us experience challenges in at least one of the following areas involved in listening: paying attention, understanding, and remembering.

You can improve your listening skills by focusing fully on someone when they are speaking. Here are some ways to do that:

- Don't interrupt the other person. Hear them out.

- Keep listening to the other person, even if you think you know what they will say next. If you make assumptions, you may miss the point they're making.

- Pay attention to the other person's nonverbal signals (tone of voice, facial expression, body language, etc.). These signals can give you clues about what the other person is thinking.

- Ask questions in order to clarify what the other person has said. Try repeating what they have said in your own words to make sure you understand. Take notes if necessary.

- Don't be distracted by outside interference. Loud noises, the other person mispronouncing a word, or even an uncomfortable room temperature can break your concentration and distract you from the conversation.

- Give feedback to the other person. Nod occasionally, say things like "I see," and smile, if appropriate. Let them know you're listening.

- Use paraphrasing. In other words, repeat back your understanding of the wishes of the client. It can help alleviate misunderstandings later on. For example, you could say: "So, Mr. Smith, would I be correct to say you envision a casual yet elegant, warm and inviting setting for your dinner party and wine tasting complete with a live jazz combo, for up to 50 guests to be held sometime between the third or fourth week of July and the middle of August?"

Reading Non-verbals

Being a skilled reader of people can not only help you get the job, it can help ensure you keep your clients satisfied. In addition to hearing what people say, a skilled event planner also notices non-verbal communication. For example, did a prospective client fold their arms when you made a particular suggestion? If so, they may be communicating that they disagree, even if they don't actually say so.

Although body language can't tell you precisely what someone is thinking, it can give you clues so you can ask follow-up questions, even as basic as "How do you feel about that?" If you want to improve this skill, you can find some excellent advice in the book *Reading People*, by Jo-Ellan Dimitrius.

Negotiation

As soon as a client or employer decides they would like to work with you, you will be faced with the issue of how much you will get paid. You will find information about standard fees for event planners later in this guide. However, no matter what fees are "standard," you may be able to get paid more through effective negotiation skills.

Likewise, being a good negotiator is a vital skill to have when dealing with vendors. Events involve contracts, and every contract involves some level of negotiation. It's important to learn how to negotiate to achieve a positive outcome for all parties.

The optimal result of any negotiation is to come away in a win-win situation for everyone. As you become more experienced and known in the events industry it will become easier for you to negotiate deals with vendors because of the volume of work you can bring them. Until you earn a reputation in the industry you will have to be a little more creative to negotiate the best possible prices for your clients. Here are some effective negotiating tips:

Negotiate with the Right Person

Do not waste your time negotiating with people who do not have the authority to give you a discount. You may get along really well with a venue sales coordinator but if the general manager is the only person with the authority to make deals then go directly to him or her.

Be Prepared

A vital part of negotiating is knowledge. If you enter into a negotiation about the price for a service without first finding out the industry average you will not know if the price the vendor is suggesting is fair or not. Do your homework and gather information on pricing and other variables from as many vendors as possible.

Be Creative

If a vendor won't budge on the issue of price try to get them to include something that won't cost them much, but will give the client perceived value. Here are just a few examples of items you can negotiate a lower price on or try to get for free:

- Price of meeting room or a free hospitality room if a certain number of guest bedrooms are booked through a hotel

- Free parking with a venue that normally charges a fee, or some free bottles of champagne if total liquor package is ordered through one vendor

- Reduction in price for a guarantee of a "block booking" (booking a certain number of guest bedrooms) at a hotel.

Come Ready to Deal

When entering a negotiation phase with a vendor be prepared to offer something in return. If the vendor is relatively new to the marketplace and trying to build a client base you could offer to pass out their business cards at your next networking opportunity. Come up with a list of ways your service is unique and can benefit theirs and be ready to use the list at the negotiating table. If you are working with clients who are influential people in your city make sure the vendor knows this.

Use Smart Negotiating Tactics

One of the best ways of ensuring you are getting a good deal from a vendor is to tell them you are shopping around and getting comparative bids from their competitors. Another tactic often used is the offer of an immediate deal if the vendor reduces their price by a certain percentage. The vendor may be willing to give the discount rather than have you leave the premises to shop around.

Finally, don't be afraid to ask for what you want. The worst that can happen is that someone refuses. After all, if you are persistent and ask for three things the vendor might just give you one and you walk away with one more thing than you started with!

Develop the ability to get people to say "yes," whether you are asking for a corporate sponsorship or a free floral arrangement. Always ask yourself "What's in it for them?" when approaching someone, and make sure you present those benefits.

There are many excellent resources to help you become a master negotiator, including the book *Getting to Yes: Negotiating Agreement Without Giving In,* by Roger Fisher and William Ury.

3.1.2 Organizational Ability

As you saw in chapter 2, event planners need to ensure that numerous tasks must be organized. The following skills will help ensure your success in keeping on top of everything involved in putting on an event:

Detail-Oriented

Seeing the big picture is important, but you'll need to be able to break that vision into smaller pieces. As the saying goes, to eat an elephant you need to start by taking a bite. Make a detailed plan of attack for your event elephant.

Have a binder or a notebook with tabbed sections on food, vendors, contracts, guests, publicity, etc., so you can easily lay your hands on the information you need. This binder should be self-contained and portable so you can bring it with you to vendor meetings and have it with you on the day of the event. Take the time to set this up early in the game, and maintain it faithfully.

The software market offers several event planning organizational tools for planning and registration. These can go a long way toward helping you stay organized and making sure no details are overlooked. You will find information about software programs that can help you keep track of event details in section 5.2.3 of this guide.

Time Management Skills

Time management skills are critical to being successful in this business. At times it may seem that there is never enough time to do everything that needs to be done to put on an event, but there are a number of ways you can manage time more efficiently if it seems you "never have enough of it".

- **Keep an activity log.** For a few days, use a notebook to jot down things you're doing as you do them, and note the time when you change activities. After a few days, analyze the log. Chances are you will notice some time-wasters. (To get real insight from this activity, make sure you don't change your normal behavior.)

- **Concentrate on RESULTS – not being busy.** If you have ever had the experience of working hard, but achieving little, it may be due to something known as the Pareto Principle, also known as the 80-20 rule. For most people, 20% of their activities lead to 80% of their results. The other 80% is "busy work" – we're doing something, but getting relatively less (20%) results.

- **Do what's important.** There are four categories of tasks based on urgency and importance:

  - urgent and important
  - non-urgent and important
  - urgent and non-important
  - non-important and non-urgent

  While it would be logical to focus first on tasks that are both urgent and important, many people spend a lot of time on tasks that are not important, either because those tasks are urgent or because they are easy. Completing a lot of easy tasks, even if they are not important, can give people a sense of accomplishment. Of course, putting off the more difficult tasks that are important but non-urgent, eventually leads to them becoming urgent!

- **Set daily goals to help you keep on track.**

- **Divide your tasks into lists based on priorities.** Your A List should be things that must get done today. Your B List is items to do only if everything on the A list gets done (e.g. errands that could be done tomorrow or following day). Your C List is every-thing else which should be done only after everything on your A and B lists has been done.

3.1.3 Creativity

The best events will offer guests something unexpected and unique. You want them to remember your event and be excited about the prospect of coming back again. Don't host a rubber chicken affair; strive for a little more creativity in your offerings or their presentation. If you've seen it a million times, so has most of your audience. So think outside the typical event box. Some ways to develop creative ideas include:

Brainstorm

Sit down with others involved with your events business, and try to come up with as many new event ideas as you can. To brainstorm effectively, make sure that there is a continuous flowing of ideas with-out any judgment and that the ideas are not discussed until all ideas have been stated. (Ideally, one person should be keeping track of them and writing them down.) When you let yourself talk and blurt out ideas without thinking about them, the most amazing and creative ideas can start to come out. After you have your list of ideas, you can then discuss them and you will be surprised at how many good ideas come out as you discuss the list.

> **TIP:**   Let yourself go when coming up with ideas — you can al-ways modify them later to come in line with your budget and objectives.

Leave a Note Pad by Your Bed

Write down any ideas that come to you as you are drifting off to sleep or when you first awake in the morning. It is proven that the brain is considered to be more creative when it is in the "Alpha" state (just before falling asleep and immediately after waking up and also while dreaming).

Read and Watch

As mentioned in chapter 2, a good way to come up with ideas for theme parties is by keeping up with what's hot on television. *Entertainment Weekly* magazine publishes top 10 lists in every issue to help you keep up with the most popular shows, movies, books, CDs, etc. Pick up an issue at your newsstand (to access their website you need to use AOL or sign in with a code that's published in each issue).

You will find a variety of resources mentioned throughout this guide, including the next section. Check out as many as you can and chances are you will find numerous excellent ideas that you can adapt.

Develop Plan Bs

It's a good idea to get into the habit of having a "Plan B" ready in case Plan A doesn't work out. As you saw in chapter 2, you can have backup plans ready in case of a crisis. However, you can't be prepared for every possible thing that could go wrong. For example, more than one event planner has received a call saying the speaker would not be able to make it. What would you do with 500 people showing up in an hour to hear the speaker?

Ask yourself "what if?" questions at every opportunity. For example, when you are at a restaurant, you might ask yourself "What would I do if I were the owner of this restaurant and the chef quit in the middle of dinner hour?" Try to think of as many different solutions as you can to a variety of problems. Doing this exercise will develop your ability to roll with the punches, so that when something goes wrong in "real life" you will be capable of quickly finding a solution. This skill goes hand-in-hand with...

3.1.4 Persistence

Beverly Ingle, an independent marketing consultant and experienced event planner, tells the following story of a near-miss at a major event:

> "In the mid-1990s, the destination management company I worked with won the contract to produce the events for the American Automobile Association's (AAA) annual convention.

As the event production manager, I was tasked with putting together, among other things, the closing party for approximately 800 delegates in my city's largest hotel.

The client requested indoor fireworks as part of the festivities. Through due diligence, I contracted a pyrotechnics contractor my company had worked with on other projects. That contractor had experience working with the city, as well. My ducks were in a row, our paperwork for permitting was ready, and all was rolling along as expected. Until the day before the event.

Both the pyrotechnics contractor and I had left numerous messages for the fire marshall regarding our plans and confirming that all would be approved, with nary a return phone call. We even faxed over the plans indicating where the pyrotechnics would be positioned in the room in relation to the stage and the ballroom's fire exits.

Fully expecting to pull the permit the day prior to the function, as was the status quo in my city, my pyrotechnics contractor headed down to the fire department's main office. The call I received at about 3:00 p.m. made me ill. The fire marshall refused to issue the permit, saying that because of the city-wide events planned during the same time, his department was short-staffed and could not properly supervise our activities.

Tourism is the Number Two industry in the city I live in, and you just don't tell AAA no. I burned up the phone lines for the next three hours, calling the fire chief, the mayor, the director of the convention and visitors bureau, the director of catering at the hotel and any other heavyweight I could think of. The bottom line: the pyrotechnics had to happen. Fortunately, the pressure from someone who these powers-that-be didn't know from Eve worked. The fire chief even admitted that his fire marshall was remiss in not returning our previous phone calls and was short-sighted in helping us produce what was an important event for our city.

The show went on with fabulous pyrotechnics that the crowd loved. And the fire marshall assigned to our event was the same gentleman who never returned our calls.

To this day, as far as I am aware, I am the first and last person to ever receive permission for indoor pyrotechnics in this city.

What did I learn? Never settle for the status quo. Pester the heck out of someone if necessary to get your permits and any other required documentation in hand well before the event. And NEVER be afraid to call in the big guns, whether you know them personally or not.

3.2 Ways to Learn Event Planning

One of the wonderful things about a career in event planning is that you have many options for learning. Unlike some professions such as accounting or engineering, there are no specific educational requirements required to become an event planner. (There are, however, some certification programs available that we will cover later in this chapter). Here are some ways to learn event planning.

3.2.1 Information Interviews

Vendors

One of the best ways to learn about all aspects of event planning is by speaking with vendors. After all, they are experts in their respective areas and most have built their businesses by servicing events.

For example, a catering company could give you detailed information and ideas for meals and snacks that are used by most event planners for different types of events (breakfast buffets, build-your-own sandwich buffets, pasta stations, etc.). They can also tell you approximate costs, how far ahead to book a caterer, what their busiest times of year are, and anything else you would need to know about catering for meetings or events.

Building a strong relationship with different suppliers is essential for success in the events industry, so it would be worth your while to set up appointments to speak with a variety of vendors. But, how do you get to know suppliers when you are the new kid on the block or have not yet met anyone from these industries?

Fortunately, there are a variety of ways to find them. Start by asking friends or family members who have recently planned an event about the suppliers they used and whether they were happy with the services of those suppliers. Almost everyone has attended an event in the last year (like a wedding, Christmas party, or festival) and hopefully can provide a contact for you to find out who the suppliers were.

Next, look for suppliers that advertise their services for events. Look in the Yellow Pages under any of the categories mentioned in section 2.5 on Vendors (e.g. hotels, party rentals, speakers bureau, etc.).

Before you set up an appointment to meet with a supplier, jot down a list of questions that you want answered and use that list as an agenda for the meeting. Here are a few good questions to get you started:

- What types of events does your company specialize in?

- What types of products do you carry?

- Do you have access to products that you don't normally carry?

- How much lead time do you require?

- How much deposit is required and when is it payable?

- When is the final payment due?

- What is your cancellation policy?

- Do you offer discounts to industry professionals (i.e. event planners)?

- Do you have a standard contract in place?

- What types of crisis situations have you seen happen and how were they handled?

- What is your best advice for a novice event planner?

Event Planners

One of the best ways to find a busy event planner to interview is through a personal referral. Ask your network of contacts if they know anyone who works in a job that involves planning meetings or events.

If possible, go beyond getting a name and telephone number. Ask the individual who personally knows the event planner to contact them, explain that you are learning about event planning, and see if you can call them to ask a few questions.

If no one in your network knows anyone who is an event planner, you can try arranging a meeting with a cold call. Grab the Yellow Pages and start dialing. Explain that you are studying event planning and ask if you can arrange to meet with them for 20 minutes to ask a few questions. People are much more likely to agree to a meeting if they know it won't take too much time.

> **TIP:** Although you are conducting an "information interview," it may be better to avoid using that term when you first call. Many professionals assume someone who wants to set up an information interview is actually looking for a job, not simply looking to learn about the profession. So they may decline to meet with you if they do not currently have any job openings. Instead, it may be better to say that you are doing research.

Be prepared that the event planner may not be available for a personal meeting but may be willing to answer questions on the phone or by email. If they make such an offer, take them up on it! If you're sending an email, you're more likely to get a response if it is limited to only a few key questions.

If the event planner agrees to a personal meeting, arrive on time and come prepared with a list of questions. At the 20-minute mark, acknowledge that your time is up, say you know they are busy, and offer to leave. If the event planner doesn't have another appointment, they may be happy to extend the meeting. (If you want to make a good impression, it's usually not a good idea to stay longer than agreed without permission.)

After asking and learning about what types of events the event planner organizes, you can ask about any area that you would like to learn more about. For example:

- How do you get people to attend your events?

- Which vendors do you work with?

- What are some challenges you've experienced and how did you handle them?

- What advice do you have for getting corporate sponsorships?

While owners of event planning businesses may also be willing to speak with you, be aware that they probably will not be eager to help if you start a competing business in the same locality. However, if you are going into a niche they do not serve, they might be more willing to tell you how they built their business.

After the Interview

Whenever someone takes time to assist you, make sure you thank them. Send a thank you note to the person you interviewed and, if someone referred you, thank that person as well. If you make a good impression, it might lead to future opportunities such as an internship or even a job.

3.2.2 Evaluate Other Events

Observation is often an excellent teacher. To observe events, attend as many different types as you can fit into your schedule. Check the Upcoming Events column of your local newspaper to find out about public events such as fairs and festivals. Contact your Chamber of Commerce to find out about business events. Say "yes" to invitations to weddings, parties, and other social events – even ones you wouldn't normally attend.

> **TIP:** To avoid paying a fee to attend costly events, contact the organizer and volunteer to help out. This will give you an inside view of the event.

When you attend the event, make note of your observations. For example, when you are registering, notice:

- What is the process for registration?

- Are there line-ups? (If so, how do attendees appear to feel about it? Are they excited to be part of such a popular event? Are they frustrated at waiting? What do you think would make them feel better about the wait?)

- Does the staff appear to have everything under control?

- Are you made to feel welcome?

- How could the registration process be improved? (e.g. more staff, fewer forms to fill out, signs telling people where to go, etc.)

To assist you in your research, consider getting a 5x7 wirebound notebook to take to events. Note the date and the event at the top of the first page, along with your other observations. Alternatively, you might prepare a sample evaluation form (see section 2.8.1 for a sample conference evaluation) and leave room for notes.

TIP: Be discreet when taking notes. It's not a good idea to whip out a notebook at a family dinner party and start writing a critique of the food. (You can expect people to be curious about what you are doing!)

Ask Others for Evaluations

Almost everyone attends events of some kind – music festivals, book signings, business conferences, tradeshows, etc. Finding people to talk to about their past experiences should not be too difficult.

Start by canvassing your family, friends and business associates for anecdotal information about past experiences, or ask them to keep a little journal for you when they next attend an event. As an alternative, you could create a short event evaluation form and ask the person attending to spend a few moments appraising the event.

Other people's opinions can give you insights on how events are seen through the eyes of attendees. You will learn what went wrong, and you may discover what people think is exciting, trendy or new.

3.2.3 Volunteer to Organize Events

Non-Profit Organizations

One of the best ways to gain experience in event planning is to volunteer on event committees for local organizations. Non-profit groups are always looking for help on their fundraisers and galas, and you'll get the double benefit of helping a worthy cause while you hone your skills. This is also an excellent way to make contacts in the community to help you land a paying job when you are ready.

You can find help in locating your community's non-profit groups through the Internet. GuideStar at **www.guidestar.org** is a searchable online database of more than 850,000 non-profit organizations in the United States. If you click on "Advanced Search" you can search by your city, state, and non-profit category (e.g. Arts, Environment, Health). CharityVillage has a similar database of Canadian non-profit organizations at **www.charityvillage.com/cv/nonpr/index.asp**.

You might also contact your local Volunteer Center or Chamber of Commerce. Both of these organizations usually run a volunteer matching program and can help make the introductions you need to get involved. Other opportunities to volunteer your services as an event planner include:

- your local community association

- your child's school

- a local nursing home

- any civic event (sports events, music festivals, parades, etc.)

Volunteering to Plan Business Events

Back in the old days, when throwing a party meant putting out a plate of crackers, cold cuts and cheese and unscrewing the top on a couple bottles of Baby Duck, almost anyone could plan a successful party. Even gala events were simple in comparison to the computer-generated sound and laser light pyrotechnical showstoppers of today.

Back then, you simply rented a ballroom (where you were assured of a nice – but perhaps stuffy – room) in a local grand hotel, booked the local favorite orchestra, let the chef decide on a dinner menu and invited the city's elite. Planning the gala event of the year (there were usually only one or two) could be accomplished quite nicely by almost anyone. Secretaries, public relations clerks and anyone else the boss could collar rose to the occasion (not always willingly) and got the job done.

There are still armies of volunteers who plan wonderful events, but most of today's workers are simply too busy to act as event planner as well. So, here's the good news — you can still get experience the old-fashioned way, by offering to plan or at least coordinate some aspects of every event you hear about.

Start at your own workplace. Most companies have at least one or two events a year (i.e. Christmas parties or summer picnics) and some have many more than that. If your company has a social committee, volunteer for it. If they don't have one, start one. If they have a public relations department that is notoriously short-staffed, offer to help them out. The beauty of this plan is that you will be learning a new career while still being paid at your old job!

If you aren't currently employed (or if you are employed, but have the time) you could offer to volunteer with special events at a spouse's or family member's place of business.

Don't Forget Events for Family and Friends

Any opportunity — yes, even unpaid — is a valuable learning experience and one where you will make contacts by networking with planning industry professionals. When someone wants to use your services, try to work with them the way you would with a "real" client, using the steps described in chapter 2.

TIP: To get the most benefit from your volunteer work, arrange to have photographs taken of all the events you are involved in planning. The photos will be proof of your event planning experience to show to prospective clients and employers. You can also ask for a letter of recommendation. See section 6.2.2 for more information about preparing a portfolio and getting letters of recommendation.

3.2.4 Internships

What They Are

An internship is a short-term, entry-level position that gives you hands-on work experience. As an intern you would go to work for a company at regularly scheduled times (although you might work as few as eight hours per week) and carry out tasks assigned by your supervisor. The main difference between an internship and a regular job is that most interns are not paid.

Although you will likely be volunteering your services to a company, you get practical work experience that can be very helpful once you start applying for jobs or start looking for clients for your own event planning business. In fact, many employers consider internships as real work experience when making hiring decisions.

As an intern you can make valuable industry contacts, learn new event planning skills, and build your resume and portfolio. You can offer your services for as little as a week; however, you will have the opportunity to learn more if you can arrange a longer internship.

Finding an Internship

If you are a student at a college or university, they very likely have an internship program or work-study program already in place.

Assuming you are not attending a college that arranges internships, there are a couple of ways to set one up yourself. First decide which companies you would like to work with. (See chapter 4 for information about different types of companies that hire event planners.) Then start calling. If it's a large company (such as a hotel chain), you can ask their human resources department if they have an internship program. If they do have such a program they will tell you how to apply.

To see an example visit the website of TCI at **www.tcico.com/pages/jobs.html**. TCI is a major destination and special event management and marketing corporation based in Washington, D.C., San Diego, California, and Austin, Texas.

If you want to work with a small company such as a local event planning firm, ask to speak with one of the owners. (Ask the receptionist, or look the company up on the Internet first, to find out the owner's name.) Whether you get through to the owner, or speak with someone else in the company, explain that you would like to volunteer your services as an intern.

While you might think any company would jump at the chance for free labor, some companies are so busy the owner may feel they don't have time to train an intern. (In a few cases an event planner may not want to help train a potential competitor, either.) So be prepared to sell yourself, using your interpersonal communication skills. Explain why you will bring value to the company.

One thing that most companies need is help doing the tasks that no one else wants to do. If you are willing to answer telephones, make photocopies, run errands, do the filing – in other words, if you are willing to do "whatever it takes" to help them out – say so.

If someone is interested in having you intern for them, they will ask you to come in for an interview and may ask to see your resume and portfolio. In many ways, applying for an internship is similar to applying for a job. You will learn more about that in chapter 4.

Making the Most of an Internship

Once you have an internship, do a first-class job with every task you are given, even the menial tasks. Everyone "pays their dues" when they are starting a new career, and those who do it with a positive attitude can make a great impression.

Look for any opportunities to get actual event planning experience—even if it means working a few more hours than you originally agreed to. Volunteer to help out whenever you can. Be someone who does such a great job that you will be missed when the internship is over. Here are some other tips for making the most of your internship:

- Don't forget to ask questions. If you are unsure about a task you have to complete, or even if you're just curious about some aspect of the event planning business, ask your supervisor. It's their job to supervise you, but they can also be a valuable source of information, as well.

- Work on what interests you. If a project comes up that you would like to work on, ask your supervisor if you can get involved.

- Get organized. Keep records of your work. Consider starting a journal of your internship activities, and try to document every project you work on for your portfolio. Keeping track of everything you've learned can help you when you apply for a job in the future.

- Set up evaluation sessions with your supervisor. This gives you a chance to ask about projects or assignments and get feedback on your performance.

- Learn what the other employees in the company are responsible for. This will give you an idea of other types of jobs in the event planning industry.

- Attend professional association meetings. Your company likely belongs to at least one; ask your supervisor about attending a meeting.

- Keep a list of networking contacts.

At the end of the internship, ask your supervisor for a written letter of reference. If you have done exceptional work, you may even get a job offer from the company you interned for.

You can find articles and a database of internships by registering at **www.internweb.com**.

Job Shadowing

For some companies, it may be easier to have you spend a short period of time with an employee than to find someone to supervise you for an internship. Job shadowing involves spending a day, a week, or some other limited period of time observing someone work.

It allows you to learn more about a career, ask questions, and actually see what a job entails on a daily basis.

Most job shadowing is arranged through personal connections, although you might be able to arrange a job shadow by calling companies that interest you.

3.2.5 Get a Part-Time Job

A good way to get related experience is by taking a part-time job for a company involved in the events industry. Even if the job doesn't focus on event planning, it can give you an opportunity to learn valuable skills that could help with your future job hunt. In fact, many prominent event planners started their careers after working for a supplier (i.e. caterer, hotel, party rental company, etc.). According to the California Employment Development Department,

> "Persons wanting to enter this field usually start by learning the meeting planning business on a small scale, often as part of a job's duties in a company. They may also work for self-employed meeting planners or as assistants to planners in associations. Some enter the field from the hotel/restaurant industry, having worked at conventions or large meetings in a variety of capacities."

One of the easiest ways to get this kind of experience is by applying for a part-time customer service or sales job. Many entry level positions have high rates of staff turnover, so companies are always hiring. While the starting pay won't be high, you will get the kind of experience that employers and clients look for. If you have the opportunity, look for a position where you will have an opportunity to work with and learn about a broad range of events. See chapter 4 for information about types of employers and tips on how to get hired.

3.2.6 Read About Event Planning

You can learn a tremendous amount about event planning, and get excellent ideas for your own events, by reading books and periodicals. Here is a selection of some of the best resources to help you become an expert event planner:

Magazines

Most of the magazines listed below have great websites that include articles and advice from their current issues and some archived issues as well. Two must-reads are *Event Solutions* and *Special Events*.

Event Solutions magazine is filled with industry news, expert advice, industry benchmarks, hot trends, success stories, case studies, and information-packed articles. *Event Solutions* also publishes yearly Fact Books and Source Books. For subscription information phone 480-831-5100 or visit **www.event-solutions.com**.

Special Events is a monthly trade magazine whose mission is to serve as a resource for event professionals. For information phone 310-317-4522 or visit **www.specialevents.com**.

Make sure you also check out these other industry resources.

- *Meeting Professionals International (MPI)*
  Phone: 972-702-3000
  www.mpiweb.org

- *Corporate Meetings & Incentives*
  Phone: 402-505-7173
  http://cmi.meetingsnet.com

- *Meeting News / Successful Meetings*
  Phone: 847-763-9050
  www.meetingnews.com

- *Meetings & Conventions*
  Phone: 303-470-4445
  www.meetings-conventions.com

Books

Most successful event planners own many books they can refer to for ideas or advice. Following are some excellent books to consider adding to your event planning library:

- *Dollars & Events: How to Succeed in the Special Events Business,* by Joe Jeff Goldblatt and Frank Supovitz

- *Event Planning: The Ultimate Guide to Successful Meetings, Corporate Events, Fundraising Galas, Conferences, Conventions, Incentives and Other Special Events,* by Judy Allen

- *Gala!: The Special Events Planner for Professionals & Volunteers,* by Patti Coons

- *Planning Successful Meetings and Events,* by Ann J. Boehme

- *Special Events: Twenty-First Century Global Event Management,* by Joe Jeff Goldblatt

3.3 Education

As mentioned earlier, no degree is required to become an event planner. However, having some educational credentials can make a good impression on both employers and clients.

3.3.1 University and College Programs

Educational programs related to event planning are typically offered through hospitality departments. A recent search at Petersons.com found 204 universities and colleges in the United States offering programs in Hospitality Administration/Management.

TIP: While any type of hospitality education may be helpful in learning about the industry or getting a job, some programs offer few courses in actually planning events. Review the course descriptions to see if a particular program will give you the education you are looking for.

Top Hospitality Degree Programs

According to the most recent rankings from the *Journal of Hospitality & Tourism Education* (December, 2002 issue), the top hospitality management undergraduate programs in the U.S. are as follows:

1. Purdue University

Located in West Lafayette, Indiana, Purdue offers a Bachelor of Science degree with a tourism specialization through the Department of

Hospitality and Tourism Management. It is designed to prepare graduates to assume management positions with employers such as hotel sales departments, convention and conference centers, cruise ships, theme parks, and resorts. For information visit **www.cfs.purdue.edu/ RHIT** or phone the undergraduate academic advisor at 765-494-8724.

2. University of Nevada at Las Vegas

In addition to a Bachelor of Science in Hotel Administration, the university offers an Executive Master's of Hospitality Administration in Meetings, Events, Conventions and Expositions. Concentrations are offered in Convention, Meeting and Exposition Management; Tourism; Club Management; Entertainment and Event Management; and Hospitality and Casino Marketing. The university awards a Bachelor of Hotel Administration degree and an Executive Master of Hospitality Administration in Meetings, Events, Conventions and Expositions. For information visit **www.unlv. edu/Tourism** or phone the Tourism and Convention Administration Department at 702-895-3930.

3. Cornell University

Located in Ithaca, New York, Cornell's School of Hotel Administration offers both Bachelor's and Master's programs through the School of Hotel Administration. While the focus is on hotels, a wide range of courses is offered including Catering and Special Events Management. For information visit **www.hotelschool.cornell.edu** or phone the Hotel School at 607-255-9393.

4. Michigan State University

Located in East Lansing, The School of Hospitality Business at MSU offers an undergraduate business degree in hospitality, with electives that include Meeting and Event Planning Management. An MBA with a hospitality business major is offered through The Eli Broad Graduate School of Management. Visit **www.bus.msu.edu/shb** or phone 517-353-9211.

5. Pennsylvania State University

Penn State's School of Hotel, Restaurant and Recreation Management offers a Bachelor of Science degree in Hotel, Restaurant and Institutional Management. Courses include Convention Management. Also offers an Associate's degree by distance learning, and Master's programs in Hotel, Restaurant and Institutional Management. Visit **www.hrrm.psu.edu** or phone 814-865-1851.

Other Degree Programs for Event Planners

The following institutions offer degree programs with courses on event planning. Many also offer certificate programs, as noted below.

> **TIP:** Universities and colleges sometimes move web pages, so if a particular link doesn't work, go to the institution's home page to do a search for the program.

George Washington University

Located in Washington, D.C., GWU's Department of Tourism & Hospitality Management offers both degrees and certificates. Degree programs include a Bachelor's of Business Administration in Sport, Event, and Hospitality Management, Master's of Tourism Administration, Online Accelerated Master's of Tourism Administration, and Master's of Business Administration with a concentration in Tourism and Hospitality Management. Certificate programs include an Event Management Certificate available by both classroom and distance learning, and a Destination Management Certificate. Visit **www.gwutourism. org** or phone 202-994-6281 for information about degree programs or 202-994-6002 for information about certificate programs.

Georgia State University

This Atlanta university offers a Bachelor's in Business Administration with a Major in Hospitality and Master's in Business Administration with a Concentration in Hospitality. A Certificate of Hospitality Administration is also offered. Visit **http://robinson.gsu.edu/hospitality** or phone the Cecil B. Day School of Hospitality Administration at 404-651-3512.

Indiana University

Located in Indianapolis, IU offers a Bachelor of Science in Tourism, Conventions and Events Management and a Certificate in Events Management. Visit **www.iupui.edu/~indyhper/tcem.html** or phone the campus operator at 317-274-5555 and ask to be put through to the Department of Tourism, Conventions and Events Management.

Leeds Metropolitan University

Leeds is the leading UK provider of Event Education. Their School of Tourism and Hospitality Management is home to the UK Centre for Events Management which offer a BA (Hons) in Events Management and Master of Science in Events Management. Visit **www.lmu.ac.uk/ ces/thm/centres_ukcem.htm** or phone 00 44 (0)113 2835937.

Metropolitan State College of Denver

The Department of Hospitality, Meeting and Travel Administration of-fers a Bachelor's in Hospitality, Meeting and Travel Administration with a concentration in Meeting Administration. A course on Meetings is offered online. Visit **www.mscd.edu/~hmt** or phone 303-556-5638.

New York University

The Preston Robert Tisch Center for Hospitality, Tourism & Sports Management at NYU offers Certificates in Meeting, Conference and Event Management and Advanced Meeting and Event Management, a Bachelor of Science in Hotel and Tourism Management with a concentration in Conference and Event Management, and graduate certificate and Master's degree programs. Online you can visit **www.scps.nyu.edu/departments/department.jsp?deptId=21** for information about certificate programs. That page also links to degree programs, or you can phone 212-998-7200.

Northeastern State University

Located in Tahlequah, Oklahoma, NSU's Meetings and Destination Management Program offers a Bachelor of Business Administration in Meetings and Destination Management which can be taken in per-son or through distance learning. Visit **http://arapaho.nsuok.edu/ ~mdm** or call the College of Business & Technology at 918-456-5511.

Roosevelt University

This Chicago University offers a Bachelor of Science in Business Ad-ministration with a major in Hospitality Management which includes courses in special events, meetings, conferences, etc. A Master's of Business Administration in Hospitality Management is also available. Visit **www.roosevelt.edu/etsuc/hosm.htm** or call the Manfred Stein-feld School of Hospitality & Tourism Management at 312-281-3172.

University of Central Florida

Located in Orlando, the University offers a Bachelor of Science in Hospitality Management with a Convention/Conference specialization through the Rosen School of Hospitality Management. The school also offers a Master's in Hospitality and Tourism Management. Visit **www.hospitality.ucf.edu** or phone 407-823-2188.

University of Houston

Rated among the world's premier hospitality education programs, The Conrad N. Hilton College of Hotel and Restaurant Management at the University of Houston offers both Bachelor and Master of Hospitality Management degrees. Visit **www.hrm.uh.edu** or phone 713-743-2255.

University of New Orleans

The Lester E. Kabacoff School of Hotel, Restaurant and Tourism Administration offers a Bachelor of Science in Hotel and Tourism Administration with a concentration in Convention and Event Management Master's of Science in Hotel, Restaurant and Tourism Administration. Visit **www.uno.edu/~hrt** or phone 504-280-6385.

You can find a complete list of hundreds of hospitality degree programs worldwide at Hospitality Sales & Marketing Association website at **www.hsmai.org/Resources/degree.cfm**.

Certificate and Continuing Education Programs

Many colleges and universities offer certificates in event planning or a related area. To earn a certificate, you must complete a number of courses. The exact number and required subjects will vary from one educational institution to another, as will the length of the program.

Most classes are held on evenings and weekends, although some educational institutions have daytime programs. In the near future, an increasing number will offer online courses as well.

The types of institutions that offer certificates in event planning range from small community colleges to well known universities, including some of those in the previous section such as George Washington University and New York University. For example, a few of the California institutions that offer certificates in event planning or meeting planning are: California State University, Cañada College, Orange Coast Community College, San Francisco State University, San Jose State University, and Sonoma State University, among others.

You may be able to find local programs by doing an Internet search for certificate program, event planning, plus the name of your city. However, new event planning programs are introduced frequently, and not all are advertised on the Internet, so if you want to get a certificate you should also contact local educational institutions directly.

Virtually every college and university has a continuing education department. If you can't find a listing for the continuing education department in your local phone directory, call the college's main switchboard and ask for the continuing education department. That department should be able to tell you if they offer an event planning certificate.

Your local college or university may offer event planning courses, even if it doesn't offer a certificate in event planning. Through the continuing education department you may be able to take a single course on a Saturday or over several evenings. Not only can this be a valuable learning experience, you can also list any courses you have taken on your resume. When you visit an educational institution's website, search for courses using these terms:

- Convention
- Event
- Hospitality
- Meeting
- Tourism

To search for colleges or universities in other cities, visit **www. petersons.com** and click on College Search.

3.3.2 Professional Certification Programs

Several of the major event planning associations offer certificate programs to designate a certain level of professional achievement. These certifications will give you the necessary credentials that employers are seeking, as well as membership in a network of like-minded professionals.

A brief overview and contact information is provided below for each.

Certified Meeting Professional (CMP)

Offered by the Convention Industry Council (CIC), this designation is based on professional accomplishments and an academic exam. It is designed specifically for persons currently working in the meeting planning industry.

Convention Industry Council
8201 Greensboro Drive, Suite 300
McLean, VA 22102
Phone: (800) 725-8982
www.conventionindustry.org/cmp/index.htm

Certified Special Events Professional (CSEP)

Available through the International Special Events Society, the CSEP designation recognizes professional achievement in the field of special events. It is earned through a combination of work experience, service and a self-paced study module and final exam.

International Special Events Society
401 North Michigan Avenue
Chicago, IL 60611-4267
Phone: (800) 688-4737
www.ises.com/CSEP

Certification in Meeting Management (CMM)

This certification, offered through Meeting Professionals International (MPI), is for executive level planners with at least five years' experience in the industry. MPI also offers two institutes, providing intensive training in events management at two levels. Institute I is appropriate for entry-level planners, and Institute II is geared toward planners with three to five years' experience. Programs are offered yearly in the fall.

Meeting Professionals International
4455 LBJ Freeway, Suite 1200
Dallas, TX 75244-5903
Phone: (972) 702-3000
www.mpiweb.org/education/cmm

Other Certifications

The International Society of Meeting Planners offers five separate designations, geared toward different specialties in the industry:

- Certified Event Planner (CEP)

- Registered Meeting Planner (RMP)

- Certified Entertainment Manager (CEM)

- Certified Destination Specialist (CDS)

- Incentive Travel Specialist (ITS)

Requirements include having completed a formal degree program, continuing education, or extensive experience in the field.

International Society of Meeting Planners
1224 North Nokomis NE
Alexandria, MN 56308
Phone: (320) 763-4919
www.iami.org/ismp

4. Getting Hired

Once you have developed your skills and knowledge of event planning, it's time to start getting paid for your talents.

While event planning is a glamorous career that attracts many people, the good news is that there are an increasing number of job opportunities. Although the government doesn't track employment rates for "event planners," according to The U.S. Bureau of Labor Statistics, meeting and convention planners are projected to have "faster than average" employment growth from 2000 to 2010. The experts interviewed for this book also report that there is plenty of work available for event planners.

This chapter begins by taking a look at the types of industries that hire event planners, followed by advice on how to find job openings, how to put together the materials you'll need to apply for a job, and how to make a great impression on an interviewer.

Throughout the chapter, you will receive advice from experts in the business on how to get hired as an event planner.

4.1 Employers That Hire Event Planners

As you will read below, there are many types of organizations that hire event planners. These employers fall into three major categories:

- Event planning companies

- Hospitality industry

- Corporate employers

4.1.1 Event Planning Companies

As an employee of one of the companies in this category, you would work on events for a variety of client companies that have hired the company you work for. While some of the companies that provide this service call themselves an "event planning company," there are actually a number of different types of companies that provide event planning services.

Incentive Houses

An incentive house (also known as incentive company) specializes in developing programs to motivate employees. For example, an insurance company may hire an incentive house to plan a trip and meeting at a Caribbean resort to reward insurance agents who have accomplished sales goals.

According to Wendy Spivak, principal of the Boston, Massachusetts-based Castle Group, sales contests are the most popular event marketed by incentive houses and "travel is the top motivator." Incentive companies offer fabulous opportunities in the event planning business due to large budgets, and the events tend to be large as well.

The Society of Incentive and Travel Executives at **www.site-intl.org** offers a variety of links and articles at their website. You can click the "Guest Access" link, or you can become a registered user of the site by completing a free registration process.

Destination Management Companies

Destination management companies (DMCs) provide local event planning services for companies that want to hold an event in a different city. They essentially handle all the details once a group arrives at their destination. They are hired for their local knowledge and resources to plan tours, meetings, conventions and other events. These companies offer a variety of entry level job opportunities, ranging from sales to hosting tours.

The Association of Destination Management Executives has information on destination management opportunities and to what's happening in the business. Visit **www.adme.org** or phone 303-394-3905. Other good sites with helpful information and links are Global Events Partners at **www.globaleventspartners.com** and Destination Management Resources at **www.dmc-net.com**. The DMC site offers a directory that lists hundreds of destination management companies.

Event Planning Firms

For variety and excitement, consider working for an established event planner. You'll learn the ropes from the ground up and gain valuable contacts.

You may find local event planning company listings through the phone directory (check the Yellow Pages under "event planners"), your local Chamber of Commerce, or by doing an Internet search for "event planner" and your city.

Although there is no complete online directory of event planners, you can find some listed at the International Special Events Society site at **www.ises.com**. Click on "Find an ISES Member."

A national event planning company to check into is **PGI, Inc**. The company creates more than 2,500 events annually, "translating client objectives and strategic messages into qualitative experiences." Founded in 1990, the Arlington, Virginia-based company employs more than 500 full-time and 2,600 on-call event and communications professionals in 32 cities worldwide. Their Canadian website has links to other offices at **www.pgicanada.com/pgi.html** or phone the world headquarters at 703-528-8484.

Marcia Bradley, General Manager of PGI in San Diego, has these words of advice on breaking into the event planner business:

> "Work at a destination management company (DMC) first. Giving events is only a fraction of what the business entails. Get into a DMC or event company any way you can. Then, make yourself invaluable so they will give you opportunities in all areas. Be an intern or receptionist or sales coordinator— whatever it takes. You've got to start somewhere and it's an easy business to move 'up' in."

Public Relation Firms

Many, but not all, public relations firms handle event planning. There is a difference between an "event" and a "publicity stunt." So do not immediately assume that every PR firm out there handles events.

According to Dianne Chase, president of A La Carte PR, located in Charlotte, North Carolina, event planning within the PR industry really "runs the gamut." Chase says that events could be anything from sponsoring a public service project such as a walk-a-thon to holding a special event for your clients.

You can find local public relations firms in the Yellow Pages (under "public relations"), by doing an Internet search for "public relations agency" or "public relations firm" and your city, or through a professional organization.

The Public Relations Society of America (**www.prsa.org**) is the professional organization for U.S. public relations professionals, while the Canadian Public Relations Society (**www.cprs.ca**) is the national organization for Canadian public relations practitioners. Both organizations have chapters across the country.

Advertising Agencies

Ad agencies, similar to public relations firms, organize a variety of events for their clients. A typical event focuses on promoting a client's products or services. Since some ad agencies only design and buy advertising, look for a "full service" advertising agency to find one that also plans events.

Like public relations agencies, you can find local advertising agencies in the Yellow Pages (under "advertising agencies"), by doing an Internet search for "advertising agency" and your city, or by getting involved with a professional organization. Online, check out the American Association of Advertising Agencies at **www.aaaa.org**, the American Advertising Federation at **www.aaf.org**, or the Institute of Communications and Advertising (in Canada) at **www.ica-ad.com**.

4.1.2 Hospitality Industry

The hospitality industry offers many job opportunities for those who want to work in the events industry and have the security of a steady paycheck. While some jobs involve planning events from start to finish, most involve providing services to other event planners or people who are planning events for an organization.

There are a variety of job titles in the hospitality industry that may include any combination of words to describe:

- an event (catering, conference, convention, event, hospitality, facilities, meeting, trade show, special events, etc.)

- a role (e.g. assistant, coordinator, director, manager, marketing, organizer, planner, producer, representative, sales, service, etc.)

For example, you may find job titles such as Convention Services Manager, Catering Director or Sales Coordinator (see the information below about Hotels and Resorts for some specific examples).

The hospitality industry also offers numerous entry-level positions that can lead to a position involved with event planning.

Hotels and Resorts

A hotel may be the site of many events – from banquets to business meetings to bar mitzvahs. If you want to work with a hotel, the department that will give you an opportunity to work with people planning events is the sales and catering department (at some hotels it may be known as just "sales" or just "catering").

A typical entry level position is sales coordinator, a job that may involve more administrative work than actually working with customers. At some hotels, the next level up is sales representative or you may just move into the position of sales manager or catering sales manager. At a single hotel, there may be several such positions. (The person at the top may have a title such as director of catering services or the director of sales and marketing.)

As mentioned in chapter 3, one way to get started in the events industry is with a part-time job. Starting as a banquet server, for example, will give you the opportunity to learn the inner workings of events, how to deal with challenges that crop up, and how to get along with co-workers and the sometimes demanding public.

Sarah Lowis, CMP, CMM, Operations Manager of International Conference Services Ltd. in Vancouver, B.C. advises people who ask her how to break into the event planning industry to "work in the hotel industry". She says,

"In a hotel, you will develop valuable skills in customer service, multi-tasking and organization. You will also meet and work with meeting planners or have exposure to the catering department and the special events they organize."

To find a job in the hotel industry, you can start by visiting the websites of hotel chains you are interested in working with. These sites list hotel locations at their website and you can apply directly to the hotel(s) where you are interested in working. You may also find a few job opportunities listed at the corporate website. Here are sites of luxury hotel chains:

- *Fairmont Hotels and Resorts*
  www.fairmont.com

- *Hilton Hotels*
  www.hilton.com

- *Marriott International*
  www.marriott.com

- *Radisson Hotels*
  www.radisson.com

- *The Ritz-Carlton*
  www.ritzcarlton.com

- *Starwood Hotels (Sheraton, Westin)*
  www.starwood.com

You can also find links to luxury hotels at the Leading Hotels of the World web site at **www.lhw.com**. Of course you can find many hotels in your city simply by checking the Yellow Pages or type your city into the Search box at **www.officialtravelguide.com**.

Another way to find hotels is by checking with convention and visitors bureaus. The site OfficialTravelGuide.com lets you do a search by city, and brings up a link for that city's convention and visitors bureau (CVB). Click on the link to go to the official page for the CVB and you can then click on accommodations or hotels to search for facilities.

Tourism Organizations

Convention and Visitors Bureaus (CVBs) act as a community's official "destination management companies" for meetings, conventions, and other events. CVBs are sometimes referred to as "tourist boards" or "tourism offices".

The International Association of Convention & Visitors Bureaus (IACVB), a professional organization with over 1,100 member bureaus in 30 countries says some of the specific services CVBs can offer the meeting planner are:

- On-site logistics and registration

- Developing pre- and post-conference activities, spouse tours, and special events

- Assisting with site inspections and site selection

- Providing speakers

- Assisting in the coordination of local transportation

IACVB at **www.iacvb.org** has more information about the industry, while OfficialTravelinfo.com lets you find a CVB near you. Visit **www.officialtravelinfo.com/mapnavigation.asp**.

Convention Centers

Convention centers usually have in-house event planners to deal with all the trade shows, conventions, and other events they might handle each year.

> The McCormick Place Convention Complex in Chicago, Illinois, hosts the Chicago Auto Show, the National Hardware Show, and the National Restaurant Association Show. Eugene Hardison is the McCormick Place's assistant director of event excellence. According to Hardison, working for a convention center (like other positions in the hospitality industry) is a bit different from being a planner for a company or association since he and his division work with other event planners to assist them in running a smooth event.

To network and keep up on industry news check out the Association of Convention Operations Management at **www.acomonline.org**. The Convention Industry Council web site at **www.conventionindustry.org** also offers links to other industry associations.

You can find local convention centers through your convention and visitors bureau (see above) or simply type the name of your city and "convention center" or "conference center" into a search engine such as Google.com. The International Association of Conference Centers lists a number of facilities at its website at **www.iacconline.com**.

Clubs

A club can be a fabulous place for an event planner to work. Clubs may host banquets, receptions, meetings, and events such as tournaments. Some of the types of clubs where events are held include:

- chambers of commerce
- country clubs
- cultural centers
- golf clubs
- military clubs
- private clubs
- university faculty clubs
- yacht clubs

Some clubs have event planners in-house while others farm out the work. If you find a club that doesn't have an event planner on staff, it may be an opportunity for you to create a job. See section 4.2.3 to find out how to create a job.

For information about the industry, visit the Club Managers Association of America (CMAA) web site at **www.cmaa.org**. Another good resource is their *Club Management* magazine.

You can find local clubs by checking the Yellow Pages or contacting your local convention and visitors bureau. To find chambers of commerce online visit **www.chamberofcommerce.com**.

Cruise Lines

Like hotel and resorts, cruise lines employ staff to help groups plan events such as conferences. These staff members typically work on dry land, although cruises can be a perk of the job. Much of the information about other land-based hospitality jobs applies to these positions as well.

Shipboard jobs that involve events are carried out by the cruise staff department. The cruise director is the head of this department and coordinates daily cruise activities. Other positions in this department are assistant cruise director, social hostess, and cruise staff. Here's a small part of what the *FabJob.com Guide to Get a Job on a Cruise Ship* says about the cruise staff job:

> "These are some of the most rewarding, fun-filled jobs to have on a cruise ship, and the entry-level opportunities are vast. Every ship has a cruise staff, loaded with talented, high-energy individuals essential to the guests' entertainment and participation in cruise activities. Your day may include lip sync contests, sock hops, pool Olympics, limbo and dance contests."

Cruise ship jobs offer free travel to exotic destinations such as the Caribbean, Hawaii, Alaska, Mexico, free room and board, plus starting salaries averaging $1,500 - $2,500 per month. The SeaLetter site offers links to dozens of cruise lines at **www.sealetter.com/resource.html**.

Vendors

Vendors that serve the events industry offer a variety of job opportunities. These positions may give you the opportunity to assist clients in planning events, or they may simply offer an opportunity to break into the industry with an entry-level job.

Section 2.5 of this guide has information about the many types of vendors involved in event planning. Working with any vendor – from florists to photographers to speakers – can help you break in and learn about the events business. Entry-level positions may include sales, customer service, and administrative support. Two vendors that may give you a good opportunity to actually work on organizing an event are:

Party Rental Companies

These companies supply a wide variety of items to people planning parties, including: balloons, bars, carriages to transport guests, casino equipment, chairs, dance floors, dinnerware, tents – just about anything that can be used to put on a party or other event. A job with a rental company can give you the opportunity to learn about many different types of events, and the special touches that can make them a big success. The American Rental Association publishes a list of rental stores, and event planning tips at **www.rentalhq.com**.

Caterers

Caterers help clients choose menus, and may also coordinate other aspects of the event. An example of what this position may involve can be seen in this Monster.com job ad:

CATERING SALES REP / EVENT PLANNER

Catering by Windows, the Washington, DC area's premiere caterer, is known as one of North Americas' leading providers of exceptional food, cutting-edge culinary creativity and outstanding presentation. The company provides full service catering, party planning and event management to meet any catering need, from corporate receptions to weddings and fundraisers to backyard barbecues. Every affair begins with an experienced and attentive event consultant, who custom designs each menu and coordinates food, decor and presentation to ensure a spectacular event.

Check the Yellow Pages or the local Chamber of Commerce's list of catering companies. Many caterers hire additional help during their "busy season" (June weddings and graduation parties, December holiday parties and during the summer). Once hired, make sure the managers know that you are interested in learning all you can about the "behind the scenes" planning for events. As you gain experience, ask if you can take on the entire planning process for one event (start small) and document your success.

For information about caterers, check out the National Association of Catering Executives (NACE) at **www.nace.net**. They also publish a newsletter called *The Professional Caterer*.

Attractions

Any place that attracts tourists (known as an "attraction") may offer a possible job opportunity for an event planner. Here are some examples of attractions:

- amusement parks

- aquariums

- casinos

- Disneyland

- family fun centers

- factory tours

- ghost towns

- historic sites

- monuments

- museums

- national and state parks

- performing arts

- professional sports teams

- raceways

- scenic trains

- theme parks

- visitor centers

- wineries

- zoos

Many attractions hold events to promote the attraction itself. For example, a zoo may hold a fundraising gala, a museum may host exhibition openings, and a winery may offer wine tasting events. From receptions for donors to open houses, many attractions hold promotional events throughout the year. In addition to such events, attractions are often used as a venue for other events – corporate team building events, family fun days, weddings, holiday parties, conferences, etc.

If a popular attraction in your community isn't currently being used as a venue for events, you could approach them and suggest creating a new department with you as the event coordinator.

Armed with the information on marketing that you will find in the next chapter of this guide, you might explain how you could help to promote the attraction to companies for events. If you can show how you will bring more revenue to the attraction than it will cost to employ you, you could create your own job! You will get tips on how to create your own job later in this chapter.

One way to find attractions is by checking websites of convention and visitors bureaus. The site OfficialTravelGuide.com has a map you can click on to find a particular destination and a link for that city's convention and visitors bureau (CVB). Visit **www.officialtravelinfo.com/ mapnavigation.asp**. Many CVBs have a link to "attractions" on their website, or you can phone and ask for information about local attractions.

You can find links to Amusement and Theme Parks, as well as Family Fun Centers at **http://members.aol.com/parklinks/links.htm**. To find links to casinos, locally or in major centers such as Las Vegas, visit Worldwide Casino Directory at **http://casinocity.com/casinos**.

4.1.3 Corporate Market

The corporate market includes corporations as well as other employers such as professional associations, non-profit organizations, educational institutions, government, and hospitals.

A commonly used job title in the corporate market is meeting planner. However a variety of other titles may be used, depending on the organization. In some organizations, event planning is done as part of another job by a staff member whose title or job might include:

- administration
- corporate communications
- human resources
- investor relations
- marketing
- member relations
- public relations

> **TIP:** Event planners who work in the corporate market can get a tremendous amount of valuable information from Meeting Professionals International, the leading industry association for meeting planners. There are 60 chapters worldwide. For information visit **www.mpiweb.org** or phone their headquarters at 972-702-3000.

Corporations

Most large corporations have in-house events staff. Sales meetings, annual board of directors meetings, training seminars, open houses, trade shows and conferences all need good planners.

In smaller companies, the event planning – such as awards dinners, holiday parties, training seminars, etc. – may fall to an office manager or someone within the human resources department.

There are a number of other places to find links to top companies in the United States and Canada. The following are good places to start your company search. At **Hoovers.com**, you can search for a specific company, or click on "Companies & Industries" to go to a page with a menu that allows you to browse a company directory or search by industries. The *Fortune* and *Forbes* sites list top companies in the U.S., while *Report on Business* lists top Canadian companies.

- *Forbes Magazine*
  www.forbes.com

- *Fortune*
  www.fortune.com/fortune/alllists

- *Report on Business*
  http://top1000.robmagazine.com

Trade and Professional Associations

The Association market offers tremendous opportunities for event and meeting planners.

Any group of people with a common interest may form an association. For example, there are professional associations of doctors, lawyers, managers, administrative assistants, public relations professionals, and many other occupations. Likewise, there are trade (or industry) associations for people who work in particular industries, such as banking, fashion, construction, travel, insurance, and many others.

Among the thousands of associations are local, state and provincial, national and international groups. Many of these groups hold an annual convention (which may be called an "annual meeting" or "conference"). They may also hold a variety of other events for their members, ranging from awards banquets to seminars.

The American Society of Association Executives site at **www.asaenet. org** has links to over 6,500 associations. You can find a list of Canadian professional associations at **www.charityvillage.com/cv/nonpr/ profas.asp**. The Professional Convention Management Association site at **www.pcma.org** is another excellent resource for anyone in North America who plans conventions.

Corporate Promotional Events

While any type of company may hold a large public event (such as the Saturn car company's weekend event for 38,000 customers, mentioned earlier in this guide), there are some companies that hold promotional events on an ongoing basis.

Retailers, for example, hold a variety of events to attract customers. Examples of such events are a fashion show at a department store, a demonstration by a celebrity chef at a shopping center, or a singles evening at a grocery store. You can find some interesting information about retailers through the National Retail Federation at **www.nrf.com**.

Media (newspapers, radio stations, and television stations) also hold a lot of public promotional events. Turn on a popular radio station on a Saturday and you are likely to hear a DJ reporting from a community event. According to Wendy Spivak, of Castle Group in Boston, media outlets usually act as co-sponsor of events such as road races and blood drives. "Sometimes, anchors will act as the master of ceremonies at these types of events," Spivak says. For a listing of major newspapers, radio stations, and TV stations, visit **www.journalismjobs.com**.

Not-For-Profits

These groups are also a huge market for event planners. Non-profits host fundraisers, galas, awards ceremonies, community festivals or other special events. Many times the development (fundraising) department or communications department handles the work, in conjunction with a volunteer committee.

More than 850,000 non-profit organizations in the United States are listed at **www.guidestar.org**. If you click on "Advanced Search" you can search by your city, state, and non-profit category (e.g. Arts, Environment, Health). CharityVillage has a similar database of Canadian non-profit organizations at **www.charityvillage.com/cv/nonpr/index.asp**.

Government

Event planners for cities organize festivals and other events for the community and to showcase the area. Event planners also work for many departments in state, provincial, and national governments. Their work is similar to that of meeting planners in corporations or associations. For example, they may plan conferences, training seminars, or public events.

To find U.S. and Canadian government departments, check the front of your phone book or visit **www.govspot.com** for U.S. sites or **www.canada.gc.ca/depts/major/depind_e.html** for Canadian sites.

Universities

Event planning for universities includes homecoming events, fundraising events and alumni activities. Event planners work in many different departments on a university campus, including the alumni association, student association, faculty club, and for large faculties.You can also search for colleges or universities at: **www.petersons.com**.

Hospitals

According to Wendy Spivak, the most common events in the medical field are community-oriented events such as blood drives, health fairs, free blood pressure testing and educational programs. The American Hospital Association provides information to help hospitals plan events for the annual National Hospital Week (held in May). An online directory of hospitals is available at **www.hospitalconnect.com**.

4.2 How to Find Job Openings

There are a variety of ways to find job openings. This section covers both traditional and non-traditional ways to find job openings, including how to create your own job.

4.2.1 Advertised Positions

Newspapers

Check the classified section of the city where you would like to work. Periodically, there will be job listings for event planners or related positions. And, don't overlook the hotel and hospitality sections. Be sure to find out if daily editions from the newspaper are available online – that will save you the price of a paper each day. To access a newspaper online, do a search on **www.newspaperlinks.com**.

Because event planners have a variety of job titles remember to look for a variety of headings when scanning the classifieds, including: catering, conference, convention, event, hospitality, hotel, facilities, meeting, trade show, special events, etc.

General Jobs Boards

The popular job sites typically list thousands of event planning jobs across the country. To see as many jobs as possible, begin by doing a search for the term "event". To find specific positions try terms such as "meeting planner". You can also search by type of employer. For example, if you are interested in working for a "resort", "hotel", "caterer", etc. you can search for that particular term.

- *Careerbuilder.com*
  www.careerbuilder.com

- *HotJobs.com*
  www.hotjobs.com

- *Monster.com*
  www.monster.com

Commit to searching the myriad of job boards at least an hour a day. Listings change from day to day and many jobs are filled within days. If you are qualified for a job listing, act quickly and send out responses to as many jobs as you are qualified for and interested in. By sheer numbers, you will find your dream job sooner the more you send out.

Industry Job Sites

While the general job boards offer the greatest number of positions, you may find the ideal job for you at one of the following job boards for the events industry.

- *Benchmark Hospitality*
  www.benchmark.hospitalityonline.com

- *MPI*
  www.mpiweb.org/resources/jobs/results.asp

- *mpoint*
  http://jobs.mpoint.com

- *Event Planner*
  www.eventplanner.com/boards/employment.html

- *hospitalitycareernet.com*
  www.hospitalitycareernet.com

- *Hospitality Careers Online*
  www.hcareers.com

- *Hospitality Jobs Online*
  www.hjo.net/Wantads.htm

- *Hotel Job Resource*
  www.hoteljobresource.com

- *International Association of Conference Centers*
  www.iaccnorthamerica.org (Click on Job Board)

- *SOS Hotels*
  http://careers.soshotels.com

You may find additional job listings by checking out the other industry publications and websites mentioned throughout this website.

Hotel and hospitality industries publish their own newsletters and magazines, as do many large CVBs. Most of these publications include a classified section where jobs (both temporary and long-term) are listed.

4.2.2 Unadvertised Positions

A study reported in the *Harvard Business Review* found that almost 80 percent of jobs are not advertised in the classifieds. That figure may be even higher for a fab job such as event planner. Even among the types of employers that usually do advertise for event planners, smaller companies may not have websites, and are unlikely to spend hundreds of dollars to post jobs at a site such as Monster.com. So how do these employers find employees?

Networking

Many employers find employees through word of mouth. When a small business owner needs a new employee, they will typically ask friends, business associates, and current employees if they know anyone who might be suitable for the job.

Many hiring managers pass resumes around. If you can network with and impress Employer A – who may not have an opening at any given time – they may be willing to pass your resume along to a company they know that is hiring. If you wish to get a job, you must get on as many radar screens as possible.

When you are ready to get hired as an event planner, it is no time to be shy. Tell all your friends, family and former business associates that you are looking for work. If you belong to volunteer organizations, be sure to mention to the group that you are now available for paying jobs. Here are tips from two successful event planners about effective ways to network for a job:

> *"Don't be shy! Talk, talk, talk about your desire to work as an event planner. And ALWAYS give out and get business cards from people you meet. When people give you their cards, be sure to follow up with a phone call or e-mail within a day or two. You don't have to ask for a job. Just remind them how you met and that you enjoyed talking with them — then, repeat your desire to break into the event planning business."*
> — Sherri Brennan

"Always show up where the people in power congregate. The more posh an atmosphere, the more likely there will be people who are in a position to hire. Get into the habit of haunting places such as country clubs, four-star hotels, great spas, exclusive salons, restaurants and bars and golf courses. It might cost you some money, but it can be worth making the right contact."
— Lynn Simpson

In section 6.3.1 of this guide you will find practical advice on how to network to find event planning clients. You can also use the advice in that part of the guide to help you meet and connect with people who can hire you – or recommend you to someone who can hire you – for a full-time or part-time event planning position.

Direct Contact

Even if you don't know anyone connected to a particular company, it may still be possible to get a job there by contacting the company directly.

It happens rarely, but sometimes a manager will have just decided that they need a new person, when they happen to receive a phone call or resume from someone who looks like they might be an ideal candidate for the job. Many employers would rather find someone this way than invest all the time and effort in advertising the job, screening resumes, and interviewing numerous candidates.

As mentioned in section 3.2.1, you can also try to schedule information interviews with professionals in the business and ask them for advice. Since someone is giving you precious time – and time is money in any business – don't push them to hire you, but rather keep in mind you're on a fact-finding mission. If the person you're networking with makes it clear that they have no openings at present, don't push it, because if they have a further opening and you impress them, you may get the call.

Other ideas can include making contact by telephone, email, or mail. If you decide to make "cold" contact with employers (as opposed to the "warm" contacts that come through networking), it's a good idea to focus on specific types of employers.

This allows you to target your job search most effectively since it takes time to track down company owners' names, tailor your resume, and prepare personalized cover letters explaining why you want to work with that particular company.

See section 4.3.2 for more about cover letters, and section 6.4.2 for tips on how to track down contact information and make cold calls.

4.2.3 How to Create a Job

Even when no job is open, someone may hire you if you can show them that you will give your employer more value than you cost. To do this, you will need to know what you can do for an employer that will outweigh the costs to the employer of hiring you. Here are some examples of things that employers see as "costs" when they hire a new employee:

- your salary

- your benefits

- resources you'll need to do your job (e.g. computer, supplies)

- time of other staff members to train you

- time of your supervisor to oversee your work

As you can see, you will need to demonstrate to an employer that you would bring them more value than simply covering the cost of your salary. Here are some examples of things that employers may see as valuable:

- increasing profits by getting more sales

- increasing profits by reducing the company's costs

- freeing up your boss's time so he can do more important work

- reducing your boss's frustration by doing tasks she doesn't like doing herself

For example, a busy event planner might hire you to be her assistant if you can convince her that, with your help, she could do more of the tasks she enjoys and fewer of the tasks she doesn't enjoy, while being able to take on more events and earn more money.

Likewise, an organization that could be used for events (such as a local attraction, caterer, private club, or rental company) might hire you to set up an "events department" if you can convince them that you can increase profits by getting more customers. Chapter 6 of this guide has many ideas on how to market a business and attract clients.

To create a job for yourself, you will need to deal directly with someone who has the authority to hire new people. This does not mean contacting the human resources (HR) department of a large company. The HR department fills positions that already exist. If you want to create a new position, you will need to speak with the appropriate department manager or, in the case of a smaller company, the owner of the company.

You will need to meet with this person and learn what they need to be able to figure out how you can create value for them. It's best if you can establish a relationship with someone through networking. However, you may even be able to create a job through cold calling. For example, here is the type of message you might leave on someone's voice mail:

> Hello (name of potential employer), this is Eva Eventplanner. I am an experienced event planner, and would like to meet with you to discuss how I could help (insert name of potential employer's company) increase profits by having me market your services to companies for events. Please call me at (insert your phone number) so we can schedule a time to meet. (If you actually reach the person, simply change the last sentence to ask when would be a good time to meet.)

If the company is looking to increase profits, as many companies are, this call is more likely to get returned than a call simply asking if there are any job openings. You may need to be persistent and make a lot of calls, but if what you are offering is something that will bring a company more value than it costs, you can create a job!

4.3 Job Hunting Materials

4.3.1 How to Prepare a Resume

Here is the good news: Even if you have never been paid to be an event planner, you can write a powerful resume that can help you get a job as an event planner.

Employers want to know you have the specific skills required to fulfill the duties and responsibilities of the position. To show them you have those skills, you will need to get some event planning experience using several of the methods suggested in Chapter 3.

Exactly what you will include on your resume depends on both the job you are applying for and your previous experience. Here are some dos and don'ts, plus sample resumes for a beginning event planner and an experienced event planner.

Sample Resume

Planner With Little Experience

Polly Planner

123 Your Street
Your City, Your State 00000
(555) 123-4567
pplanner@abc.com

Objective

Seeking a position in the events/meetings industry where my experience and enthusiasm for planning events will contribute to the overall success of the organization.

Professional Experience

2002—Present
Humphrey's By The Bay (Restaurant and Concert Venue)
Administrative Assistant
- Proficient in Microsoft Office applications such as Word, Excel and PowerPoint. Other training with Access, MSN Project, PageMaker and PhotoShop
- Typing (60 wpm), filing, writing letters, answering phones
- Assist manager with details for the concert series schedule (summer)
- Greet performers and arrange for special requests

2001—2002
The Elegant Buffet (Catering Services)
Server/Setup Assistant
- Arrived prior to event to set up tables, dishes and decorations
- Helped plan menus and themes
- Served foods and beverages to function guests
- Identified potential problems and suggested solutions to insure a successful event

2000—2001
Beach Bay Cafe
Deli Worker/Cashier
- Prepared and served lunch and dinner menu items
- Assisted in preparing boxed lunches for large groups
- Ordered food and supplies for owner
- Responsibly handled the cash register and banking chores

Education

A.A. Office Management, 2002
San Diego City College

Currently enrolled in Certified Special Events Professional (CSEP) program. Certification to be completed by November 2004.

Volunteer Experience and Service

Coordinator for Annual Awards Dnner
St. Augustine Church

Program Chair
San Diego Rowing Club

Volunteer Driver
Meals on Wheels

Resume Dos and Don'ts

- **Do** include all pertinent information. Experience or training in public relations, marketing, retailing, or customer service naturally dovetails with the duties of an events planner, so be sure to highlight those. If you have attended seminars conducted by event planners' organizations or local Visitors and Convention Bureaus, by all means include that information as well.

- **Do** include information on relevant non-paying event planning experience. Planning your local Cub Scout annual dinner for the past four years may not sound so glamorous to you, but to hiring managers, that practical hands-on experience can be as valuable as extensive educational degrees.

- **Do** include professional affiliations and certifications. This includes membership in event planning associations (listed in the Appendix). Certificates can be attractive on your resume from any relevant area of interest or expertise. For example, if you take a program through the local or state Parks and Recreation Departments, find out if they offer a certificate.

Sample Resume

Experienced Event Planner

Paula Planner

12345 Your Street
Your City, Your State, 12345
(555) 123-4567
pplanner@abc.com

Objective

Seeking a position in the events/meetings industry where my eight years of experience in meeting management and communications will contribute to the overall success of the organization.

Professional Experience

1998—Present
Betz Research & Trading Inc., Orlando, FL
Meeting Manager and Marketing Coordinator
- Successfully manage and execute all educational programs, customer appreciation and employee events (20-30 annual events both local and throughout the United States).
- Develop, plan, negotiate, contract and manage all aspects of Betz's meetings and events, following through with on-site management and post-meeting reporting.
- Research and conduct site visits to determine qualification standards for our meetings and events.
- Plan and negotiate menu selections, audio/visual requirements, entertainment and ground transportation with contracted property and/or vendors.
- Create and design promotional materials, brochures, registration forms, evaluations, instructor presentations and other marketing items as they relate to the events planned.
- Manage relationships with sponsoring associations, customers and vendors.
- Arrange individual travel for instructors, CEO, managing directors, and our sales force along with coordinating group travel for customers for special events.
- Proficient and knowledgeable with Microsoft Office applications such as Word, Excel and PowerPoint. Training with Access, MSN Project, PageMaker, PhotoShop and Illustrator.

Key accomplishments:
- Designed, implemented and maintained a budget procedure for our marketing department and for all of our meetings and events, demonstrating ROI and benchmarking post-meeting reports for national meetings and events.
- Developed, managed and continuously improved meeting planning position by creating Request for Proposals (RFPs), site selection guidelines and forms, meeting specifications, contract addendums, rooming lists, meeting history and expense management.
- Managed the creation and implementation of a quarterly newsletter publication for educating bank portfolio managers.
- Created and have maintained national and state sponsorship for continuing educational credits for certified public accountants.

1995—1998
The Solution Inc., Palm Village, FL
Executive Assistant to the President
- Provided administrative management to president and sales staff.
- Scheduled meetings and corporate travel arrangements.
- Created, maintained, organized and tracked all documents and reports.
- Maintained accurate customer billing and assisted with accounts payable and receivable and bookkeeping.
- Communicated and verified business and sales information.

Professional Organizations

1998—Present
Active member of Meeting Professionals International
American Management Association Educational Programs

Education

B.A. in Marketing, 1999, University of Orlando

Awards

Company Values Excellence Award, 2001

Volunteer Experience and Service

1998—Present
Special Events Chair
Orlando Chapter of Charitable Services

- **Don't** include extraneous information. Some employers make a decision about a resume within seconds, so a resume containing too much irrelevant information could be rejected before the employer has even finished reading it. Mentioning personal information such as marital status, number of children, or hobbies you enjoy in your spare time mark you as a novice.

- **Don't** go back further than 10 years on your resume unless you have something exceptional (such as a job with Disney). Some employers judge anything you learned or did more than a decade ago to be outdated.

- **Do** ask someone (preferably in the event planning industry) to review your resume before you begin your search.

- **Do** choose an attractive paper stock, lay it out nicely, and make sure there are no typos. You are applying for a job where appearance matters. But...

- **Don't** get too fancy with your resume. One employer told us she received a resume packed in confetti; another said she thought she was receiving an expensive (and free) designer scarf when it happened to be a resume instead. Wendy Spivak adds "Don't send me chocolate with your resume."

- **Don't** stretch the truth. If you indeed orchestrated the entire annual dinner dance for 5,000 people while working for XYZ Corporation, then say so. But, if you actually only negotiated the contracts for the food vendors for that event, say that. That experience is valuable in itself and stands out as a useful, transferable skill to prospective employers. Always assume that the person in charge of hiring will check all information on your resume.

TIP: For general resume writing advice visit **http://resume. monster.com**.

4.3.2 How to Prepare a Cover Letter

If you are submitting your resume by mail, fax or e-mail, include a cover letter.

While it's okay to photocopy your resume, your cover letter should be personalized and explain why you are a good candidate for the job. To see what to do – and what not to do – in a cover letter, here are a couple of sample letters prepared in response to this job ad:

> **ABC Company, an international association of more than 1,250 insurance and financial services companies, is currently seeking a Meeting Planner. Responsibilities include acting as a meeting manager for approximately 25 domestic meetings per year; coordinating registration, printing, audio/visual setup, menus, and expenses; developing a Request for Proposal; and maintaining relationships with ABC's clients, purchasing agents, suppliers, and venue personnel. Please send cover letter and resume to hr@abccompany.com.**

Sample Letter 1

Dear Sirs:

I saw you're ad. This is the kind of job I've been looking for. I'm pretty sure I would enjoy it and it would be good experience for me. I've already sent out a bunch of resumes without much luck so I hope you'll hire me. As you can see I have everything your looking for. It's your loss if you don't hire me. Call me at 555-1212.

Polly Planner

In the cover letter above, Polly has done a number of things wrong. See how many of these mistakes you noticed:

Incorrect Salutation

Polly could make a better impression by addressing the letter to the appropriate hiring manager by name. If you don't know who to send your letter to, you can access the company website and look for the appropriate person. If this tactic is unsuccessful, you can call the event planning department at the particular company and ask who the appropriate manager is, then address your letter to that person.

Even if the advertisement reads "send letters to human resources," don't address the letter to "Human Resources." Send your letter to the decision maker because, nine times out of ten, the decision maker is going to be the person you would eventually work for if you get hired.

In most cases the human resources department screens applicants, so go directly to the source. The worst thing that can happen is that the manager of the appropriate department or division will forward your materials up to human resources. It's worth a shot.

If there is no other way but to address your letter to human resources and you don't know the gender of the person you're sending the letter to, then avoid gender salutations such as "Dear Sirs," and rather write "Dear Sir or Madam."

What's the Position?

The letter doesn't state what position Polly is applying for. Many companies advertise more than one position at a time. Omitting the position demonstrates carelessness.

Typographical and Grammatical Errors

Letters must be proofread before being sent. You'll never hear a compliment on an error-free resume or cover letter; they're supposed to be perfect. While there's no correlation between good spelling and intelligence, nothing turns off a prospective employer more than a sloppy resume. The attitude is that a sloppy resume equals an employee that doesn't pay attention to details.

Furthermore, don't rely too heavily on your word processor's spell check since it won't catch mistakes such as using "two" instead of "too." Ask a friend to read the letter for you — the most difficult part of proofreading anything is catching your own mistakes.

Failing to Address the Company's Needs

The letter doesn't address the company's needs that are clearly written in the advertisement. Polly writes that she wants to "enjoy the job and get experience," instead of directly addressing what the company wants. Employers want to know what value you will bring to them.

Employers are also very concerned with results. The major focus of the job experience section of your resume should focus on what the results of your efforts were — it should not be a rehash of a job description.

Failing to Mention the Company by Name

Polly could make a much better impression by doing a little research in order to say something flattering about the company. You can find out what a company prides itself on by checking its website. The best place to start would be in the "About Us" section.

Negativity

By stating, "I've already sent out a bunch of resumes without much luck," and "I hope you'll hire me," Polly sounds desperate. Employers may wonder if there's a good reason why no one else has hired her. And as you can imagine, writing something such as, "It's your loss if you don't hire me" does not make a good impression.

If you were an employer, wouldn't you be more impressed with the following letter?

Sample Letter 2

Ms. Jane Doe
Vice President, Event Planning Division
ABC Incorporated

Dear Ms. Doe:

In response to your [Day, Month, Date] advertisement in the Tribune, I'm writing this letter to offer myself as a candidate for the position of event planner with ABC Incorporated.

Having read the mission statement on your corporate web page, I find that our professional personalities and goals for service, dedication and excellence are closely aligned.

As you will see in my resume, I have previous experience as an event planner with an established client base that I've grown since my tenure with XYZ Corporation. In fact, the last three events that I've planned have come in 10 percent under budget. I offer these skills to ABC Incorporated.

My experience and education make a strong recipe for success with ABC Incorporated. I excel at customer service, can multi-task, and have numerous letters of recommendation.

I would be thrilled to meet with you or one of your associates to discuss my candidacy for event planner with ABC Incorporated at your earliest possible convenience.

Thank you and I look forward to hearing from you soon.

Best,

Polly Planner

This letter addresses what Polly has done and what she can do for ABC Incorporated. Your own cover letter will of course depend on the position you are applying for and the company you are applying to. It should also include your name and contact information at the top of the page.

4.3.3 Other Materials

Portfolio

A portfolio is a collection of samples of your work that you take to an interview. A portfolio can help you stand out from other applicants. It offers an employer proof that you have the skills to do the job.

Working as an event planner gives you a perfect opportunity to create a portfolio. As you gain experience in the field, your portfolio will build. If you don't have a portfolio—get busy and create one. Section 6.2.2 explains how to create a portfolio even if you have no previous paid event planning experience.

Letters of Recommendation

Including one or more letters of recommendation when you submit your resume can help you get called for an interview. Recommendation letters can be particularly important when you don't have a lot of paid event planning experience on your resume.

A glowing letter describing how impressed someone was with the work you did organizing an event for a charity can give you a huge advantage over other applicants.

People qualified to write letters of recommendation can be former work supervisors, co-workers, teachers or professors, board members from organizations you have volunteered with, professionals in the event planning field, or as a last resort, friends and family members.

Letters of recommendation should be on high-quality paper and typed in a readable font. Copies are fine. Keep a file just for letters of recommendation so they stay clean and fresh. Try to keep them as current as possible, updating with new ones as you receive them.

It is great if you can get a letter of recommendation "customized" to a specific job position, but that is not always necessary. Most skills required are transferable from other settings and situations. As long as the letters are positive, hiring managers can identify that the skills you have can be used in varied job duties.

> **TIP:** Be certain that should a hiring manager call the writer of the letter of recommendation, his or her response will be a good one. Things change. Sometimes a person who was happy to write a glowing recommendation will have cooled on their opinion of your work as time passes. Especially if you have not worked for that individual for some time, be sure to call them first and get an assurance that they will still speak of your work in the best possible light.

Business Cards

Hundreds of software programs offer templates for you to create your own business cards. Spend some time creating a readable, stylish business card for yourself that clearly spells out the services you offer as an event planner. (See section 5.2.3 for tips on creating business cards.)

Carry these cards with you always—and don't be shy about handing them out! You never know when a casual conversation may lead to a job opportunity.

4.4 Interviews

4.4.1 What Employers Are Looking For

One key thing to remember through the interviewing process is that the company seeking a new employee has a need. Interviewers are hoping that the "perfect" candidate is out there somewhere and that the company needs will quickly and relatively painlessly be filled by you—the applicant.

Of course employers are looking for someone who will do an excellent job. But they are also seeking someone with certain character and personality traits. Here are some specific traits that can help you get hired as an event planner:

"Having passion, knowing about our company, and having something to say. Tell me you've looked at our website and found it fascinating. Don't say, 'I looked at your website briefly.' That makes me think you didn't think it important enough to read. The best candidate came in with a list she'd made by looking at our competencies and then listing how she could add value! When you're asked why you want to work for a company, don't say (as one did), 'I really need a change.' No offense, but what you need (to do) is to convince me you've got something no one else can give this team."
   – Marcia Bradley, General Manager
     PGI, San Diego

"In my position I negotiate contracts for the hotel with event planners. People who do this type of work—either the events planner or the hotel's representative—must be extremely detail oriented. They have to be good listeners, understand the needs of the group, follow up on all inquiries, and never, never, never wait for a client to call you back with missing details. If a person doesn't have these qualities, it is a disaster waiting to happen because not knowing the precise details of an event is what causes catastrophes."
   – Sherri Brennan, Account Director
     Sheraton Harbor Island, San Diego

"I'm impressed when someone shows excitement and en-
thusiasm for the position."
> – Wendy Spivak, principal and co-founder
>   The Castle Group, Boston, MA

"Employers are looking for people who are resourceful, dedi-
cated to getting the lowest price, who can be creative, multi-
task and find new ways to present events."
> – Dee Suess, Division Manager
>   Banner Professional, Schaumburg, IL

Specific qualities that Lynn Simpson, an independent event planner, is looking for in potential employees includes these:

- *an ability to think on your feet*

- *an outgoing personality and confident demeanor*

- *being adept at crisis management*

- *having good social skills*

- *having the ability to improvise*

4.4.2 How to Prepare and What to Wear

The success of an interview often depends upon the amount of preparation done. So how do you go about getting prepared for the first interview?

- Confirm where the interview is being held and when. A botched appointment may keep you from your dream job.

- Read the job description or find out the skills needed for the job. (Most job ads list specific skills that are needed.)

- Decide exactly what you liked and disliked about your past jobs so you can determine if this job will be a fit for you.

- Determine your personal key achievements (how you made a difference) and be ready to describe them.

- Know your resume and letters of recommendation inside out.

- Use the Internet to research the company, the industry sector and the company's competitors.

- Conduct mock interviews prior to your appointment. Enlist the help of a trusted friend to act out the part of the interviewer. Give your friend a list of possible interview questions, and go through the whole interview—from the first smile and handshake to the last thank you. (Sample questions and answers are included later in this chapter.)

- Choose your interview clothes in advance.

What to Wear

Many job searchers have the impression that the "rules" of what to wear to an interview have greatly relaxed through recent years, but actually, the rules remain fairly conventional. The classics still apply if you want to make a good first impression. The more conservative the position and the organization, the more conservatively you will want to dress.

If the company is a more relaxed or small business, you may want to consider "lightening up" your clothing—gray or navy separates may be the right choice in this case. However, even in the seemingly relaxed atmosphere of event planning, always err on the side of formality. There will be many days to wear more casual dress after you land the job. Marcia Bradley General Manager of PGI, San Diego puts it this way:

> "Having just gone through a round of interviews for sales account executive positions, I would tell you 'safe' is better than sorry in terms of what to wear. Wear a suit. Unless the company clearly states that you can come in casual attire, I would not. Why? Even though I might not notice or care that you are wearing flip flops and a jean skirt, someone else in my office may notice. This happened just this week and my team came to me to say not to hire that person. Even if you are told casual is okay, I'd overdress!"

Of course, there are always exceptions to the rule. If you are applying for work in a totally laid back environment (a small Hawaiian island company that works off a beachfront for example), the best advice is to either drop by the company and see what all the employees are wearing—or call and ask!

> **TIP:** An important tip if you are traveling to an interview: Pack your interview clothes and accessories in your carry-on luggage. Don't let a delay in getting your baggage ruin your chances for your new career.

Tips For Women

- Choose a dark two-piece suit or a tailored dress with a jacket.

- Hose should be a neutral color, not match your suit.

- Limit jewelry and wear conservative makeup and hairstyle.

- Rather than carrying a purse, slip your essentials into your briefcase.

Tips For Men

- Choose a dark two-piece suit (lightweight wool preferred) or a sports jacket and coordinating dress slacks.

- White long-sleeved shirts are the accepted first choice. Pastel-colored shirts are suitable in a more relaxed business setting.

- Be clean-shaven or well-trimmed if you have facial hair.

Tips For Both

- Appear neat and clean.

- Buy the best quality clothing you can afford.

- Highly polished shoes still make a strong impression.

- Apply just a hint of fragrance, if any.

- Practice wearing your interview clothes until you are comfortable in them. Your focus should be on the interview and interviewer, not adjusting your new clothing.

4.4.3 How to Make a Great Impression

First of all, remember that they are interested in you. If you were not qualified for the position (at least on paper), they would not have called you for an interview. From what they have seen so far, you fit the company's needs. Accept that, and then go on to show the interviewer that you possess all the qualities that make up their definition of a fabulous employee.

You're on time, well groomed, knowledgeable of the position and the company—but you have to do one more thing. Setting the tone of the interview is, to an important extent, all up to you.

Keep it in mind that many interviewers do not like this process any better than you do. Managers who are unused to conducting interviews may feel nervous or uncomfortable. But, whether they are an "old pro" or a novice at interviewing is less important than how you conduct yourself.

Take the initiative. From the moment you are called into the room, be as confident as you possibly can be. Be the first one to make eye contact, smile, extend your hand, and introduce yourself. Speak clearly, neither too loudly nor too softly.

Be outgoing and enthusiastic. This isn't always easy because interviews can make people nervous, and nervous people tend to smile less, and act more stiff and formal than they normally would. However, as an event planner, you will be working with many people. The employer wants to see that you are comfortable even in a potentially uncomfortable interpersonal situation such as an interview. If you tend to be stiff and uncomfortable during an interview, it is time to perform. Act how you would if you did not feel nervous. This may feel unnatural at first, but behaving as if you are not nervous can actually make you start to feel that way as well.

Be inquisitive. If you have done your research on the position, the company and the industry, you will be eager to ask questions. Don't derail the tempo of the interview, but if the moment seems appropriate, be sure to jump in with a question. To the interviewer, this will show that you care enough to have done some thinking about the position and that you would be an asset to the team.

Talk about the job at hand. All too often, our experts tell us that prospective employees spend too much time asking about promotions and management positions when they should be discussing the job they're under consideration for. Focus on what value you would bring to the company as an employee, and not on what you want to get from the job. For example, don't discuss how much vacation time you want or bring up salary until the employer does.

Be assertive but not aggressive. The company probably has more than its share of "yes people" and people who just coast along. If the opportunity avails itself, don't hesitate to express your opinion on a work-related issue or concern. Taking the initiative to broach a subject with confidence will show your leadership potential and will underscore your confidence and ease with others.

Be positive. Avoid saying anything negative, especially about former employers. Also avoid saying anything negative about yourself, which some applicants do by sounding as if they are desperate for a job. Before the interview, remind yourself how much you have to offer an employer, and that there are many opportunities for you. Believe that if this particular job doesn't work out, there is something better out there for you. Exude confidence, poise, leadership, and capability. Chances are, you'll get that second interview—and your dream job!

4.4.4 Interview Questions

Standard Questions to Expect and Answers to Give

You can expect to be asked standard interview questions such as those on the following pages. It's a good idea to prepare some answers before the interview so you are able to answer tough questions. Here is a list of common event planner interview questions with suggested answers from our panel of experts.

Why Do You Want to Work For Our Company?

Prospective employers do not want a cookie cutter answer. Do your research, read the company's website and give them an answer that demonstrates that you have done your homework. "Having read your company's mission statement, I find that your business philosophies closely mirror my own" is a good way to begin your answer. Then give some specifics.

What Drew You to a Career in Event Planning?

Here, the employer is looking for the reasons you decided to pursue a career in event planning. "For the money" is not a good answer. But "I like versatility, working with people and the challenges it offers," would serve you well.

What Are You Doing Now?

The employer wants to know if you're currently in the business and, if so, they'll want to know if your current duties and responsibilities match those of the position you're applying for. Explain how your current duties relate to the job you are applying for. Also remember to mention any current volunteer experience that relates to the job.

What Kind of Position Are You Looking For?

The employer is trying to get a feel for what interests you in a position. "A position that offers growth possibilities and challenge with an industry leader," is a fine answer here.

What Did You Like Most About Your Last Job? Least? Why?

Now the interviewer is trying to discover what you don't like. If you didn't like a certain responsibility at your previous or current job, and this responsibility is required at the job you're applying for, you could get passed over. But you have to be honest if you want to find a job that you will love.

What Are Your Strengths and Weaknesses?

Focus first on answering your strengths—that's usually easier to answer. Think about the duties and responsibilities of the job and answer accordingly. For instance, "My ability to come in under budget is my greatest strength."

Avoid talking in terms of weaknesses. Instead, turn the statement into a positive one, by pointing out a personal goal you'd like to meet or an achievement you'd like to earn. For example, instead of saying you have trouble managing your time, you could state that one of your goals is to take a time management seminar to make sure you are maximizing your potential. That answer tells the interviewer two things. First, you have the strength of character to recognize a weakness; and second, you have the will to do something positive about it.

What Experience Do You Have With _____?

Depending on the company, they may want to know your experience with event planning, budgeting numbers, customer service, working in teams, supervising, juggling many projects at once, etc. Give specific examples from your experience. Include any work experience, volunteer work, internship, or education that demonstrates your skill in a particular area. For example, if you haven't done much budgeting for real events, but earned an A in an accounting class where you had to prepare budgets – tell the interviewer. This is your opportunity to show that you know your stuff.

Where Do You See Yourself in Five Years?

Sometimes employers ask this because they want to know whether you are looking at their company for long-term employment or simply a short-term job "until something better comes along." Other employers want to judge your ability to plan for the future. Most employers do not want to hear that in five years you hope to be retired or plan to start your own event planning business. "In five years, I'd like to have an advanced degree and hold a management position in this company," is a good answer.

How Do You Feel About Overtime?

Overtime and odd hours are part of event planning; it's not a nine-to-five job. What you need to know, as the prospective employee, is how much overtime the company would be asking for and if you're willing to make that kind of time commitment.

Do You Have Any Questions For Us?

"Yes!" is the appropriate answer here. Take your time and do some research so you can ask very pointed questions. Interviewers want an interview to be interactive, not just them sitting behind a desk spouting corporate rhetoric. Some standard questions you might ask are:

- What would your expectations for me be during the first six months on the job?

- What is your department/division's current business plan and how would I fit into that plan?

- What is it about your company that differentiates you from your competition?

- What are you looking for in an employee?

Aside from those standard questions, you should also surf the company's website — specifically the "About Us" section or wherever you can find press releases. The company's annual report is also a good place to get information — especially the first page, which is usually a recap of the previous year.

Find something current the company is doing or has done and ask questions on that subject. For example, "I read in one of your press releases that your revenues are up 10 percent due to increasing inter-national customers. Was this part of a specific business plan and would this affect the way your department conducts business?"

Behavioral Questions

Also be prepared to answer behavioral questions. These are ques-tions that ask you about an experience you had in the past, and re-quire you to answer with a specific real-life example. The interviewer might ask: "Tell me about a time you experienced conflict with a co-worker. What happened, and how was it resolved?"

The interviewer will not be satisfied with a hypothetical answer about what you "would" do in such a situation. They want to hear about an actual time you experienced conflict. The purpose is not to see if you have ever had a conflict (they expect you have); the purpose is to see how well you resolve difficult situations and, if something did not work out in the past, what you learned from it.

Since you are applying for an event planning position, you can expect to hear behavioral questions such as:

- Describe your most successful event so far. What did you do to make it a success?

- Describe an event where something went wrong. How did you solve the problem?

Other Questions

You can expect interviewers to ask a variety of questions based on the position and their personal preferences about what they want in an employee, for example:

> *"What is it about your personality that makes you a good event planner?"*
> – Dianne Chase, Pesident
>   A La Carte PR, Charlotte, NC

> *"How do you define being a member of a team?"*
> – Eugene Hardison, Assistant Director of Special Events
>   McCormick Place Convention Center, Chicago, IL

Prepare and practice answers to these and as many other questions as you can brainstorm. If you are asked something you haven't prepared for, try to answer as honestly as possible. This will help ensure the position is a good fit for what you are looking for.

Plus, interviewers say they are turned off by applicants who tell them what they think the interviewer wants to hear. It's okay to say "I don't know," just don't make a habit of it.

You can find more advice on preparing for an interview and answering standard interview questions online at **http://interview.monster.com**.

4.4.5 Discussing Salary

One of the touchiest questions that come up in an interview situation addresses salary expectations. Many times employers want to know right from the start what you are looking for, to rule out anyone who is completely out of their league. While this can be a time-saving approach for the interviewer, it isn't best for you.

If you are applying for an existing position, then human resources has already budgeted a specific salary range for the position.

If you are the first one to mention a specific salary figure, and it's lower than the one the employer had in mind, you risk getting hired for less than they might have been willing to pay you.

If at all possible, avoid discussing salary on the first interview. And don't bring it up yourself (it can create the impression that you are more interested in the pay than the position). If the potential employer asks you about salary expectations, it is perfectly acceptable to be polite but vague. "I'd rather wait to discuss salary until we both have a better idea of how I would fit this position," or similar wording, can help you get out of a sticky spot.

The second interview is the more appropriate time to discuss salary. Ideally you will receive a formal job offer, complete with salary and benefits package, and you can use that as your negotiating point. If there is a certain range of compensation that you feel you must receive, be upfront with the hiring manager without being demanding. And remember to use your negotiating skills to get to "yes" on both sides.

With the recent economic downturn, many job hunters are considering lower-paying jobs than they might have in the past. But don't sell yourself short. Know the industry, do your homework, and have a realistic ballpark in mind.

Typical Salaries

In their 2002 Salary Survey (the latest figures available at publication), *The Meeting Professional* reported that the average salary for a meeting planner, in US dollars, was just over $60,000 — up from $54,613 in 2001 despite a slowdown in the economy.

Salary ranges vary by job description, size of company, scope of responsibility, level of experience, region, and the type of business or organization you are working for. Government positions tended to be the best paying, while religious organizations came in lowest.

About 45 percent of workers earn straight salaries, while the balance earns salary-plus-commission, bonuses, fees, mark-ups, and/or hourly compensation.

Entry level incomes will be lower, of course, but the median salary ranges below will give you an idea of what type of annual salaries to work toward. SOURCE: *Event Solutions*, January 2003 (based on 2001 reported income)

Job Title	Rate
Director of Marketing	$53,281
Marketing Assistant	$30,161
Director of Events	$50,918
Food & Beverage Director	$45,024
Event Manager	$40,110
Director of Convention Services	$45,864
Director of Catering	$47,281
Catering Sales Director	$42,200

The following figures show average salaries based on experience. SOURCE: "Money Matters," by Blair Potter, *The Meeting Professional*, May 2002

Less than 3 years	$42,695
3-5 years	$51,245
6-9 years	$55,903
10-14 years	$61,501
15-19 years	$64,153
More than 19 years	$85,068

Use these numbers as a guideline when considering your salary expectations, and be realistic about regional differences and the current economic climate. An excellent source for regional salary information is Salary.com. This site offers industry figures from all over the United States and includes other free information as well.

While effective negotiations can lead to a higher salary, if you really want an unlimited potential for income, then you should consider being self-employed. In the next chapter you will learn how to start your own event planning business.

4.4.6 Following Up

Tips from Employers

"Be assertive when following up — don't be afraid to ask when the employer is making a decision."
  – Dee Suess

"A thank you note is good enough, don't call and torture me."
– Wendy Spivak

"I'm looking for something eloquent. Restate your skills and what separates you from the competition."
– Dianne Chase

Following up after an interview can be as important as the interview itself. Within 24 hours after the interview, follow up with a thank you letter or e-mail to the person or persons you interviewed with.

Sample Thank You Note

Ms. Jane Doe
Director, Event Planning Division
ABC Company

Dear Ms. Doe:

I just wanted to thank you for taking time from your busy schedule to meet with me today to discuss my candidacy for event planner with ABC Company and to notify you that I'd be thrilled to continue the interviewing process.

I feel my current level of education and experience is a great match between my career goals and your company's current event planning needs.

Remembering during our discussion that it's part of your company's current operating business plan to decrease budget spending by five percent by the end of your current fiscal year, my expertise in budget management would greatly assist in attaining that goal.

If you require any additional information, please do not hesitate to contact me by either phone or e-mail.

Thank you and I look forward to hearing from you soon.

Best,

Polly Planner

Your thank you note should achieve three things:

- thank the interviewer for their time

- state whether you do or do not wish to continue the interview process

- make one final sales pitch as to why you're the right person for the position

You can use your computer's software to make personal letterhead with your name and contact information.

4.5 Getting Promoted

Summer jobs, internships and part-time jobs at hotels, restaurants, theme parks and attractions can provide income and experience, but not always a viable career opportunity. So what if you find that you are really good at what you do, you like the people and the atmosphere at your job, and you want to pursue your career at that company? Well, you need to:

- Speak up. If you want management to be watchful of career opportunities where you are working, you must make them aware that you want to advance.

- Be highly visible. Make sure the management team knows who you are.

- Find a mentor. Find someone with more experience than you and learn from them. If they're good at what they do, there are reasons for it.

- Don't settle for the status quo. Being creative gets noticed.

- Take on more responsibilities. Become the expert on at least one aspect of your job.

- Always present the highest quality work ethic. Be early, stay late, solve problems.

- Start taking classes that are related to that industry. And let your supervisor know you're doing so. (You'll find a list of industry associations that offer classes in the Appendix of this guide.)

5. Starting Your Own Business

As a self-employed event planner, you can enjoy freedom and the potential for much higher income than you might earn as an employee. If you dream of having your own event planning business, the information in this chapter will give you resources and information to help you get started.

5.1 Getting Started

Before you can get to the fun part of having your own event planning business, there are a number of not so fun, but very important, matters to be handled. Before we get into the details of what needs to be done, here are some resources that can help you get started. First, here are some good resources for starting a business:

- **SCORE**
  Service Corps Of Retired Executives has volunteers throughout the U.S. who donate time to mentor small businesses free of charge. Visit their website for helpful information or call 1-800-634-0245 to find the nearest SCORE counseling location. Visit **www.score.org**.

- **Small Business Administration**
  The SBA is an excellent source of free information for anyone starting a business in the U.S. To learn about SBA business development programs and services, call the SBA Small Business Answer Desk at 1-800-U-ASK-SBA (827-5722) or visit their website at **www.sbaonline.sba.gov**.

- **Nolo.com Small Business Legal Encyclopedia**
  Nolo is a publisher of plain English legal information, books, software, forms and a comprehensive website. Their website also offers free advice on a variety of other small business matters. Their products are available in bookstores across the U.S. Visit **www.nolo.com/encyclopedia/sb_ency.html**.

- **Online Small Business Workshop**
  The Canadian government offers an Online Small Business Workshop which includes information about taxes, financing, incorporation, and other topics. Visit **www.cbsc.org/osbw**.

- **ChamberBiz**
  The U.S. Chamber of Commerce website offers free information on preparing a business plan, incorporating, choosing your office location, and other aspects of starting and running a business. Phone 888-948-1429 or visit their website at **www.chamberbiz.com/bizcenter/startup.cfm**.

5.1.1 Creating a Business Plan

Business planning involves putting on paper all the plans you have for your business, including:

- The services you will provide

- Where you will locate your business

- Who your clients are

- Who your competitors are

- Where you will find vendors of products and services

- What you will charge for your services

- How you will advertise and market your services

- How much money you will need to get started

If you enjoy being spontaneous, you may be thinking you'd prefer not to do much advance planning. However, if you are seeking financing for your business from a bank or other lender, they will expect to see a business plan that shows you have a viable business idea with an excellent chance for success. Even if you don't need financing, putting ideas on paper will give you the "road map" of where you want to go with your business and how you are going to get there.

After reading this chapter, and the next one on finding clients, you will be able to start creating your own business plan. It is a document you will probably read repeatedly as you start to operate your business.

A business plan can also help you avoid costly surprises. If you are considering whether to leave a secure job to start your own business, a business plan can help you determine the resources you will need to start your business and decide when the timing is best to get started.

Your Services

For event planners, a key component of your business plan will be deciding what services your business will offer. Here are examples:

Full Service Event Planning

Full service event planners are involved in all aspects of planning and coordinating events. As you saw in Chapter 2, the tasks you may be responsible for range from developing the theme to budgeting and scheduling to finding vendors. In addition to planning before the event, you will be available throughout the entire event to assist with any last minute details that arise.

Meeting Planning

Meeting planners specialize in planning conferences, conventions, trade shows, and other business meetings.

Special Events

Special events are typically large events that are open to the public, such as fairs, festivals, and fundraising events. The event planner may handle everything from the coming up with the theme to arranging for sponsorships.

Social Events

Your company might focus on planning events for private clients. You might plan events of all kinds or specialize in dinner parties, children's birthday parties, reunions, etc.

Destination Management

As mentioned in chapter 4, DMCs provide local event planning services for companies that want to hold an event in a different city. They essentially handle all the details once a group arrives at their destination. They are hired for their local knowledge and resources to plan tours, meetings, conventions and other events.

Incentive Travel Events

Also mentioned in chapter 4 was a type of event planning company known as an incentive house or incentive company. These event planners specialize in developing programs to motivate employees. For example, an insurance company may hire an incentive house to plan a trip and meeting at a Caribbean resort to reward top employees.

Other Specializations

Virtually any aspect of event planning, and any type of event, may be a specialization. For example, some event planners specialize in one component of putting on an event. They may offer event registration services, on-site event coordination, or event marketing. Some offer event consulting services and provide advice to people who want to organize their own events. Others specialize in types of events based on clientele. For example, some event planners specialize in corporate events. There are also specializations in particular types of events such as sporting events.

Once you have finished this guide, you should have a sense of which types of events, and which event planning activities most interest you. You can use that as a starting point for developing your business plan.

Other Parts of Your Plan

The other parts of a business plan (such as how much you will charge and how you will market your services to clients) are covered later in this chapter and in chapter 6. As you read through those sections, make notes of what you would like to do with your own business.

Because it will take some time and some investigation to create your business plan, you may learn things that change your mind about how you will set up your business. You may come up with ideas that are even better, or decide to make some changes to ensure you have a greater chance of success.

As previously mentioned, the SBA offers an extensive selection of information on most business management topics. Online, they offer "The Business Plan – Road Map to Success" at **www.sba.gov/starting/indexbusplans.html**. This information is also available in print form in the "Resource Directory for Small Business Management." For a free copy contact the nearest SBA office, which you can find listed in the U.S. Government section of your telephone directory.

5.1.2 Choosing a Business Name

Your business name needs to do several things. It must:

- Describe what you do

- Be easy to pronounce

- Attract customers

- Be unique

- Be available

To choose a name for your event planning company, start by taking a look in the phone book or on the Internet to see the names that other event planners have chosen. Notice which names stand out.

When you hear a name like **Bravo Productions** (a California-based company that organizes corporate events throughout the U.S.) doesn't it conjure up a vision of events that people will love? Likewise, **A Perfect Production** (the name of a successful Lake Oswego, Oregon company) sounds like it offers events that will be, of course, perfect. You might consider choosing a creative name, like the owners of **Cosmo Cool Concepts**, a leading party planning company in Houston. Or you might choose a name that communicates what your company does, such as **Extraordinary Events** (an event planning company with offices in California, New York, Florida, and Nevada).

When you've decided on a few names that sound fabulous, let some friends and colleagues know what you're thinking of calling your business, and ask for their comments and opinions. The decision is still up to you, of course, but the instant reactions of "real people" can be a good indication of whether you are on the right track or not.

In most jurisdictions, if you operate under anything other than your own name, you are required to file for a fictitious name. It's usually just a short form to fill out and a small filing fee that you pay to your state or provincial government.

Before registering a fictitious name, you will need to make sure it does not belong to anyone else. You certainly wouldn't want to spend your initial investment money, only to find out you couldn't legally operate under a name you had chosen because someone else owns the trademark. You can do an online search of the federal trademark database to determine whether a name has already been registered. For good advice on trademarks and other matters to consider before choosing a business name visit the **Nolo.com** site mentioned earlier.

Most start-up businesses do not bother to trademark their names because it can be costly and time-consuming. However, if your company name is truly unique, you might want to consider it. You can try doing it yourself, or hire a lawyer to do it for you.

5.1.3 Legal Matters

Your Business Legal Structure

A business can take several different legal forms. Which one you choose will have an impact on how much it costs to start and run your business. The sole proprietorship is the least costly way to go into business, but it doesn't afford some of the legal protections of a corporate structure. Here are the characteristics and benefits of various legal forms a business may take.

Sole Proprietorship

If you want to run the business yourself, without incorporating, your business will be known as a "sole proprietorship." This is the least expensive way to start your own business. It is also the easiest because it requires less paperwork and you can report your business income on your personal tax return. One drawback to this type of business is that you are personally liable for any debts of the business.

Partnership

If you want to go into business with someone else, the easiest and least expensive way to do this is by forming a partnership. Legally, you would both be responsible for any debts of the company.

Working With a Partner

A good partnership requires a bit of planning if it is to run smoothly. You may want to have an attorney set up a legal partnership, spelling out what each partner contributes to and takes out of the business. Whether or not you form a legal partnership, talk with your partner and decide:

- What tasks each of you will be responsible for

- How you will make the day-to-day decisions of the business, and how you will break a tie

- What percentage of the business each will own

- How you want the business to grow in the future

- What expectations you have of each other

It is better to find out the areas where you need to compromise before you open the doors. For example, one of you may want to have an event planning business as a fun part-time job, while the other wants to work full-time and eventually build a business that will employ other people.

During your discussions you can learn if there are any areas where you need to compromise. You can avoid future misunderstandings by putting the points you have agreed on into a written "partnership agreement" that covers any possibility you can think of, including one of you leaving the business at some point in the future.

Corporation

Whether you are working alone or with partners, if you want a more formal legal structure for your business, you can incorporate. Incorporation can protect you from personal liability and may make your business appear more professional to some clients. However, it usually costs several hundred dollars and there are many rules and regulations involved with this type of business structure (among other requirements, corporations must file articles of incorporation, hold regular meetings, and keep records of those meetings). Many new business owners consult with an attorney before incorporating.

Limited Liability Company

A Limited Liability Company is a new type of business legal structure in the U.S. It is a combination of a partnership and corporation, and is considered to have some of the best attributes of both, including limited personal liability.

The resources at the start of this chapter have further information on business structures. Excellent advice is also offered at the Quicken website at **www.quicken.com/small_business/start**.

Business Licenses

If you are planning to sell wholesale items, you will need a business license as well as a resale number (covered in secion 3.2 on Vendors). Call your city hall to get the location of your local Occupational License Office, where you will purchase a home occupational license. This is a license to work from home.

You will need to fill out your business name and phone number, and give some details on the nature of your business. Most questions on the form you will fill out are designed to detect and deter people who will be a nuisance or a risk to their neighbors, and will not apply to you. This license should cost you about $100, and will be valid for one year. You will provide a photocopy of your license upon entrance to wholesale shopping establishments.

If you are not planning to be a wholesaler, you may not need to get a business license. You can find information about getting a city business license from your city hall. You may also be required to have a county or state license so be sure to check with regulatory agencies in your area to determine what you'll need. Check the resources mentioned in the first part of this section or see the SBA's webpage at **www.sba.gov/hotlist/license.html**.

5.1.4 Insurance

Big businesses carry insurance on their property, its contents, the paperwork, their receivables, and even their employees' lives. You probably won't need to go that far. Property insurance is the first thing you need to worry about, but you may later want to consider some other forms of insurance, including disability insurance for yourself to partially replace your income if necessary.

Types of Insurance

Property Insurance

Property insurance protects the contents of your office. The cost for insuring the office equipment will probably be relatively little, and may even be handled as a rider to your homeowner's or renter's insurance. Because a lot of what you produce is "intellectual property," you might want to inquire as to how the insurance company you are considering regards paper; bills, invoices, designs, plans you've discussed with a client and written out, etc. You may be able to add a rider to your policy to cover the cost of reconstructing these things if something happens to your office.

Errors and Omissions Insurance

This type of insurance may be useful if problems come up because you neglected to do something, thinking the client was going to do it instead. Or if you forgot to insert a liability disclaimer in a contract to buy wetsuits for a scuba expedition, and the wetsuits turned out to be defective, this sort of insurance could be useful as well.

Insurance for You

If your family depends on your income, consider life insurance or disability insurance. Other types of personal insurance include health insurance or dental insurance (if you're not covered under a spouse's plan). Most people have some form of life insurance, but many do not have disability insurance, even if someone else employs them. It is an important form of insurance to consider, however, when you are solely responsible for your income.

You may be able to find insurance through membership in your local sales or sales executive associations. But anyone who is self-employed can find several types of relatively affordable insurance, as well as other small-business assistance, from the National Association for the Self-Employed.

NASE has independent agents nationwide, so you will have access to local experts on small business insurance needs. And best of all, they are small businesspeople themselves, as they are contractors – not employees – of NASE. Visit the NASE website at **www.nase.org** or phone 1-800-232-6273 to learn more.

There are other types of insurance, and many different levels of coverage are available for each type. An insurance broker (check the Yellow Pages) can advise you of your options and shop around for the best rates for you. Or you may be able to get insurance through a professional association you belong to.

5.2 Setting Up Your Business

5.2.1 Location

The first thing you will need is a place to work. Your choices include working from home or renting space. Many event planners choose to work from home when they start their businesses because it saves on the cost of an office.

Working from Home

For many people, the biggest benefit of working from home is the end of the commuter lifestyle. You can take breaks when you need them, and on those breaks you can do what you need to do, from making up the bed in the guest room to playing with Fido.

Another big plus: you can deduct from your income taxes a percent of your mortgage payment and property taxes (or rent) and a share of utilities and maintenance costs. There are various methods to make those calculations, but by far the easiest – and most acceptable to the IRS – is to use an entire room, and to use it for no other purpose.

In the U.S., IRS Publication 587 has information on how to compute the calculation and file the deduction. You can download this information by visiting the IRS website and searching for the publication numbers from the search engine on the front page. (See the section on taxes later in this chapter.)

The other thing you should check before deciding on an office at home is local zoning. Most places won't have a problem with a home-based business that adds only a few cars a day to the automobile load on your street. Most will, however, prohibit you from posting a sign in your front yard, which is okay anyway, as you will not get any clients from drive-by traffic. To find out the rules in your area, look up "zoning" or "planning" in the local government section of your phone book.

In addition to any legalities, working from home requires some planning with family members. Set regular office hours that you will insist on, both for your own focus and to keep family members from intruding when you need to work. It will be tempting for the family to interrupt you. So make it clear you are at work unless it's an emergency. (The garage on fire is an emergency; sis needing to know where the cookies are is not.)

Finally, before deciding to set up a home office, make sure you have all the space you will need to run an event planning business. You will need:

- A large desk, preferably with enough space for a phone, your computer, vendor catalogs you use most often, and plenty of writing room

- Storage space for supplies

- Space for assembly (e.g. of decorations)

- Room to expand to accommodate an assistant when you get to that point

- A couple of guest chairs, and, if space and money permit, a conversation area with comfortable chairs and table to consult with clients

Decorate your space like an office, but don't spare the office amenities, such as coffee, tea or soft drinks, and even cookies to go with them. Strike a balance between homey and professional, but make it lean toward the professional side (i.e. no plastic toys on the floor, and set meeting times when you can have a babysitter or family member care for the children out of the business area.)

Renting Space

While a home office works well for many event planners, others prefer to rent a separate space. If you find it challenging to stay motivated, or tend to get easily distracted when you're at home, an office may be just what you need to help you focus on business. A separate space also creates a better impression if you plan to have people visit you. If you want a place to meet with clients and vendors, or work with employees, you might want to consider getting an office outside your home.

Look for a place that is convenient to get to from your home, and that gives you quick access to any services you may need. Such services might include your bank, suppliers of materials, even a good coffee shop! Pick an area that suits your needs and fits your budget.

5.2.2 Telephones

You'll notice this section is titled "Telephones" rather than simply "Telephone." That's because many event planners have more than one phone. You'll need:

- A business line

- A fax line

- A cell phone

- A dedicated computer line (DSL) or a cable Internet connection

Other lines you may need later include an extra line for an employee, or just an extra line for yourself if you find you must be on the phone with a vendor and a customer at the same time. You will eliminate a lot of "telephone tag" when you are trying to arrange a difficult purchase.

Your Business Line

Your main phone number should be a business line. It will cost a little more than a residential line, but you will be listed under your business name in the white pages and under directory assistance (which makes it easy for clients to find you) and you can receive a free listing in the Yellow Pages under "Special Events" or "Event Planners".

Make this phone off-limits to the rest of the family. And always be sure it is answered professionally with the name of your business and "How can we help you?" These days, even large corporations have their phones answered by voice mail systems, so it should make little difference to your business if you either install an answering machine or subscribe to the voice-mail services offered by telephone companies.

The advantage to the answering machine is that you can monitor calls as they come in, and defer responding if what you are currently doing is more crucial than answering the phone. The advantage to the voice mail services is that they are often much easier to access from the road than an electro-mechanical box sitting on your desk (which also might develop repair problems you wouldn't know about until you got back), and they offer a number of choices about how callers can leave messages.

You could also hire someone to answer the phone when you are not there. But unless you have other work for that person to accomplish, that would certainly be a lot less cost-effective than using any of the electronic helpers available. And fortunately, answering services – with real people taking messages – are just about a thing of the past. Often, the person answering the phone would not be interested in projecting the kind of image your business should project. You can control that by putting your own message on your answering machine.

When you sign up for your voice mail or telephone service, be sure you can get an instant list of all the calls you've received since you last picked up messages. Many people don't speak clearly, or even make a mistake when they leave their voice message, and you might not be able to call them back. If you have a list of all the numbers of those who left messages, you can easily figure out which is the missing link, and call that person back. Most telephone company voice mail services offer call display, either standard or as an add-on.

Several phone companies, like Verizon, MCI, AT&T and Sprint, offer that service and you can review them at their respective websites. You can **compare rates** for service from many companies in your area at sites such as **www.LowerMyBills.com** and **www. 8884dialtone.com**.

Additional Phones

You can use your regular business line for faxes, or you can use your Internet line by installing software that lets you send faxes from your computer. (However, that poses a problem: What do you do when the fax is a document that isn't in your computer, and you don't want to scan into your computer?) While it is a bit more expensive to have three lines – phone, fax and Internet – those costs are minimal in comparison to the business you might lose if you had to explain, "Well, to receive a fax, I'll have to be off the phone. So just phone to tell me when you're going to fax it."

Even if you do have a fax line, you might consider getting the software you need to fax things from your computer to a fax receiver, in case there are times you just want to send documents totally through cyberspace without using paper. For an example of a program that does this, check out WinFax Pro.

When you install your initial business phone lines, consider making the first line a rollover line that can handle two phones. That way, when there is a call on one, the next incoming call will roll over to the other phone, which your new assistant can pick up instead of having the call go to voice-mail.

You should also get a cell phone as soon as possible. As a successful event planner, you will spend a lot of time away from your office at events, as well as investigating new vendors, and meeting with clients. While you may not be able to return all calls while you are on the road, you can pick and choose. The cell phone, coupled with a voice mail service and message forwarding, may help you increase your potential client contacts better than any other method.

Telephone Tips

Often, people will wait only a short time for a return call before they move on to the next company that provides what they want to buy, whether that's tires for their car or a consultant to help them plan an event.

So make sure you honor that callback time frame everyone seems to have. For some, it's only a few minutes. Most will wait at least half a business day, however, and you should be easily able to make contact with those callers and present your business services before they have looked elsewhere.

What about call waiting? It's rude, pure and simple. Callers these days are used to leaving messages. And if someone is on the phone with you, they don't want to be asked to hold in the middle of their important conversation unless your building is on fire.

So don't get call waiting, or, if it comes in the package of services from your telephone service provider, don't use it. It's actually easier to ignore than a ringing phone. Your caller may hear a little beep as the other call tries to kick in. But if you ignore it, the caller you're speaking with will be happy, and will also think, "Wow, I'm so important, she ignored another incoming call for me!" Don't get call waiting just to impress your customers that way, though.

Likewise, do not answer your cell phone while speaking with a client or prospect at their office, or yours. (Don't answer your desk phone, either). The only exception to that would be if, during your conversation, an opportunity arose in which you could say, "Let me call the vendor, and I'll find out for you right now" and the vendor says they'll call you back in five minutes. That makes it imperative to get a cell phone with caller ID — the only call you want to pick up in five minutes is that vendor's call, and caller ID will let you do that.

Your cell phone should have a vibrate mode, too, so you'll know if a call came in while you were meeting, and you can then check your messages and call back after the meeting.

5.2.3 Equipment and Supplies

What is that telephone going to sit on? Not your kitchen table. So you will have to furnish your home office and buy basic office supplies.

Supplies

Office Depot and Staples are everywhere, but you can also order what you need by phone and online. And depending on the order, delivery is available.

In addition to the usual office supplies, you may need specialized supplies for event planning, such as a CD player, easels, laminator, sign holders, or long reach stapler. One source of specialty supplies (nametags, etc.) for event planners is PC/Nametag. Phone 1-877-626-3824 or 1-608-845-1850 or visit **www.pcnametag.com**.

You should also create a list of basic supplies to take to events, such as: box cutter, calculator, clips, extension cords, first aid kit, markers, masking tape, name tags, paper, pens, receipts, scissors, stapler, and tool kit.

You will also bring anything else related to the specific event. This will vary depending on the event, but might include items such as copies of contracts in a binder, change for people paying at the door, credit card slips and imprinter (available from your bank if you become a credit card merchant), handouts, posters, registration list, signs, etc.

Furniture

Both retailers mentioned above offer good prices on new office furniture. And locally, you can probably find a used or discount office furniture store. But, especially since you are in a creative business, you might want to consider the home office furniture sold by two trendy lifestyle stores, Pier One and Ikea.

Pier One has myriad stores everywhere. Ikea has fewer, but they do have a great catalog – both paper and online – and they ship. Of the two, Ikea offers more in the way of home office furniture, and it's inexpensive. You can get a computer desk, chair and lamp for under $150, and it will be stylish in a Scandinavian modern way.

Pier One doesn't have office suites, but it does have occasional pieces that can be useful in home offices, from chairs (like inexpensive director's chairs to use as guest chairs) to entertainment centers and wardrobes you might find useful for your purposes.

Computer and Software

If you don't have a computer, you should consider buying or leasing one for your business as soon as you can afford it. In addition to the computer, it's a good idea to get a printer, something to back up your files (such as a Zip drive or CD-RW), and a digital camera (or a regular camera and scanner) to take and send electronic photos of events you have planned.

Many computers already have the basic software needed to run a business. Some versions of Microsoft Office come with a whole suite of small business tools. You may also want to get a bookkeeping program such as Quicken or Quickbooks as well as a database program to keep track of your clients. The MS Office Small Business Suite has one, or you can buy a database program such as ACT! or Filemaker Pro.

The staff at a computer store or your office supplies store can give you more information about specific programs and help you decide which ones are best for you.

There are a number of professional event planner software packages available. Although costly, you may find one of these programs helpful to your business.

- Event Planner Plus has been a leader in the planning software market for many years. It costs $495, and is available online at **http://certain.com/Products** or by calling Certain Software at 888-237-8246. Certain Software also produces Meeting Planner Plus for multi-day, multi-session events. At $1,995, those who specialize in conferences might consider it after being in business for a while.

- Blackbaud Software offers RE:Event, a complete event planning program that includes planning tools, online registration and a tie-in to its fundraising software, Raiser's Edge. For information phone 1.800.443.9441 or visit **www.blackbaud.com/solutions/eventplanning.asp**.

- CVent is an online event registration and marketing tool that can help you manage your guest list, and provide feedback and data analysis. Check it out at **www.cvent.com**.

If you're not yet able to afford event planning software, you can make do without it, or try a free online service such as **www.EZEventPlanner. com** which includes task tracking, e-mail reminders, timetables and an online storage site.

Photocopier

This used to be considered optional equipment for small businesses. But today, when you can get a unit that is a combination photocopier, fax machine, scanner, printer, and telephone for a few hundred dollars, you should consider getting one. You are unlikely to need dozens of photocopies; you might need to make a copy or two of an agreement from time to time, and if you have the equipment right there, you won't have to go all the way to Kinko's to do it.

And remember, time is money, especially when you have a lot to do and a lot on your mind. This business is fun, so keep excess stress as far away as you can — consider buying one of these things.

Calculator

A good desktop calculator or adding machine can make your job easier. One that makes it easy to calculate percentages would be nice. A credit-card sized calculator is nice to have in your briefcase, too, for working out charges on the spot. You might even want to consider getting a small calculator that prints. These actually do come sized to fit into a briefcase, and having a paper tape of your calculations might come in handy later when you need an answer to a cost question for a client.

File Cabinet

You'll need to organize and store information you receive from vendors and keep files for each client and event. Lateral filing cabinets are terrific. They are easy to use and more attractive, usually, than the standard metal two- or four-drawer variety. But they are expensive, so you may want to just get serviceable cabinets to begin with and hold off on the lateral files until you make more money.

Stationery

Stationery is more than just a "supply." Your stationery will present you. Although these days we use e-mail more often, you will still need stationery for confirmation letters, inquiries from vendors, and reasons you cannot imagine right now.

You can print stationery right from your computer, and many people do. But consider this: you are in a creative business. It would be better if you had beautiful, coordinated stationery, envelopes, bills/ receipts and business cards to promote your business whenever anyone receives something in the mail from you. And you might also consider adding to that a simple bi-fold brochure that describes your business and services.

Beautiful stationery can help reassure prospective clients that you have a good eye and that you can make their events look beautiful, too. Consider using heavy textured papers, raised printing, and a professional design. Check around for prices at print shops or office supply stores.

If your start-up finances are limited, you might want to consider getting free business cards from VistaPrint. They offer color business cards on heavy paper stock, and a number of different designs are available. In return for the free cards (all you pay is shipping, which starts at around $5) they print their logo and "Business Cards are free at VistaPrint.com" on the back of the card near the bottom, so you still have room to write something on the back if you want to. If you don't want anything printed on the back, you can get 250 cards for only $9.95 plus shipping.

This is a terrific value, and they are fast about getting the cards to you. Be sure if you do this that the design you choose (one of many standard images provided by VistaPrint) coordinates with your stationery, or the design you have stored in your computer to print as letterhead each time you need to send a physical document rather than e-mail.

5.3 Employees and Contractors

You may be working on your own when you first start your business, but at some point you could decide to hire people to work with you. For example, you might hire an assistant or someone to help market your company. You might hire these people as employees, or you might sign them on as contractors (self-employed business people).

You may also need to hire other contractors from time to time, depending on the event. For example, if you want to construct a special set for an awards banquet, and are not able to find just the right item from a rental company, you might hire a carpenter to do the job.

5.3.1 Employees versus Contractors

Legally, if you hire an employee, you will have to pay payroll taxes on that employee, and probably make unemployment and worker's compensation contributions to the appropriate government agency. On the other hand, you can train those employees the way you like, and you can require them to do their work at certain hours and at places you choose.

If you hire contractors, those people will have learned their job skills elsewhere. They can choose how and when to do the work. You mutually agree on what product will be delivered or what services will be performed, as well as where and when they will be performed. But you cannot require them to be at your office or anywhere else for a certain number of hours daily. It is often best to spell out what you expect and what the contractor is to do or deliver in an agreement.

Other differences between an employee and a contractor are:

- Employees work only for you. Contractors may have other clients as well as you, and can work for any and all of them.

- Employees are paid on a regular basis. Contractors are paid per project.

- Employees work for a certain number of hours. Contractors set their own hours, as long as they get the job done. That can be great for them if they are really fast, or not so great for them if they are really slow. As long as the project is finished on time to specs, it's great for you. (On the other hand, if an employee is slow, you may end up paying more salary to get the job done in overtime, or even hiring temporary help to get things finished.)

- Employees can be fired or quit. Contractors can't be fired in the usual way while they are working under contract. You may decide to have them stop working on a project, but you will be obliged to pay them according to your contractual agreement unless you are able to renegotiate the contract or successfully' sue them if you are unhappy with their work. (Of course that would only be in extreme cases; it is best to avoid lawsuits altogether!)

Even though you are not writing paychecks to contractors, but rather checks for contracting fees, there are still tax considerations. For more information about employment taxes, contact the IRS or Canada Customs and Revenue Agency.

Before you hire, check with your local department of labor to find out all the rules and regulations required as an employer. There may be other state and federal rules and regulations that may apply to you, including: health and safety regulations, Workers' Compensation, minimum wage and unemployment insurance. Check the resources provided at the start of this chapter for excellent advice on hiring employees and contractors.

5.3.2 Tips for Working with Contractors

You are ultimately responsible for how well contractors do their jobs, so you will need to find people you can depend on to do the job right, by the agreed upon deadline, for the agreed upon price.

To help you choose contractors, make appointments to meet either by phone or in person. Ask what services they provide, their rates, and their availability. For example, if you will need carpenters, it is wise to find out if they are available on short notice, if they can only fit you in on weekends, and what will happen to your project if another project they are working on ends up taking more time than they expected. You need to know that you can depend on the contractor, and that they will be willing to work overtime if necessary to keep their agreements with you. (Unfortunately, some busy contractors consider deadlines to be "suggestions" rather than requirements.)

As the event planner it will be your job to supervise them and ensure they get the job done. Remember your name (not the contractor's) is on the line if you bring in a contractor and they don't come through in a timely or professional manner or within cost. So look for someone reliable, and have at least one back-up for each job.

Wherever possible, get agreements (e.g. for costs, delivery dates, services to be provided) in writing. Also check if the contractor holds liability insurance, which covers both them and you if the client's property is damaged, or the work is not satisfactory.

Before working with a contractor, check their references. It is also advisable to contact the Better Business Bureau to find out if any complaints have been lodged against them or their company. To locate a BBB anywhere in the U.S. or Canada visit **www.bbb.org**.

5.4 Financial Matters

5.4.1 Start-Up Funding

If you begin your business as an event planner in your own home, your start-up costs can be almost nothing. Because you are spending your clients' money, you can get a deposit from them to cover purchases, or it may be possible for the vendor to bill them directly. You may also be able to get local vendors to send you items "on approval" for your clients to look at before buying. (See section 2.5 for more information about working with vendors.) However, even if you don't have upfront costs for merchandise, you may have other costs, such as promotional costs and office expenses. If so, you will need some working capital until the fees from your clients begin rolling in.

Many entrepreneurs are optimistic about how much money they will earn from their business, and that's a good thing. Set your goals high. But don't be as optimistic about how quickly you will earn it. While you may be tremendously successful right from the start and exceed your own expectations, it is wise to be prepared for the possibility that it may take longer than expected until your business earns enough to support you. A standard rule of thumb is to have six months' living expenses set aside beyond your start-up costs. Or you might consider remaining at your current job and working part-time on your event planning business until it is established.

Depending on the start-up costs you calculate in your business plan, you may find you have all the money you need to get started in your savings account (or available to spend on your credit cards). If your own resources won't cover all the things you would like to do with your business, you will need to look for financing.

One place to look for financing is from family members. They may be willing to invest in your company or give you a loan to help you get started. To avoid any misunderstandings, it's wise to get any agreements in writing even with family members.

If you decide to approach a bank for a business loan, be prepared. They will want to see a loan proposal that includes these five things:

- How much money you want

- How long you want the money (i.e. the term of the loan before repayment)

- What you are going to do with the money

- How you will repay the loan

- Collateral (assets you could sell to repay the bank if you don't have enough money to make the payments)

When you prepare this document, ask for a little more money than you need. No matter how good their business plan is, most people underestimate the amount of money they need. It is very difficult to go back to the bank and get more money when you've just gotten some. So get all you need at once, even if it seems like more than you need.

5.4.2 Keeping Track of Your Finances

If you are one of those people who seldom enters checks you've written into your check register, now is the time to get over it, at least as far as your business goes. Here are some tactics to use to keep track of your business income and outgo, and keep it separate from your own money.

Open a business account at a bank, trust company or credit union, even if you are using only your own name to do business. And use this only for paying the bills of the company and your own salary, which you then deposit in your personal account.

Get a style of business check that requires you to record checks you've written. And avoid using electronic payments. You want to create a paper trail for your business account so you are able to:

- Prove your deductions at tax time

- See at a glance where your money has gone

- Create balance sheets that your vendors or other financial institutions may request from time to time

Also, keep track of your accounts receivable, accounts payable, and so on in a ledger book, which you can get at any office supply store. Or else use an electronic bookkeeping package. The most popular bookkeeping software for small business is Quicken. For under a hundred dollars, Quicken's Premier Home and Business program will help you prepare invoices, manage your accounts, and generate reports from your records.

Finally, keep two additional ledgers – small enough to carry in your purse or briefcase – so you can log (1) mileage (or other travel expenses), and (2) everything you spend during the day (remember to keep personal and business expenses separate).

Also carry an envelope so you can keep receipts for everything you buy. The cup of coffee you buy for a prospective customer, the latest issue of an event magazine, the mileage you travel to a client's office, the pack of paper you pick up at the office supply store, the admission charge for a trade fair — these and many other expenses should be accounted for so you can minimize your taxes. And, of course, knowing exactly where your money is going will help you plan better and cut back on any unnecessary expenses. So make it a habit to ask for a receipt for every expense related to business.

Be sure to re-file these at night in the appropriate files in your file cabinet. The business receipts should be stapled to the order form for each purchase/service for a client. No matter how you design a system, make sure it works for you and that you can find receipts for anything at any time without calling in a psychic to help you figure out where you put it.

5.4.3 Taxes

Even before you begin making a profit, you've got to think about taxes. You will have to think about your own income tax, payroll taxes on any employees you hire, and, if you are incorporated, a corporation tax.

Tax Returns

If your business is a sole proprietorship or partnership in the United States, you will file a Schedule C with your personal tax returns. You'll also have to file a form to determine the amount you owe on your social security. (Canadians will do the same with CPP.) If you are self-employed, the amount of FICA or Social Security taxes you'll pay on the same amount of income doubles because when you were employed, the employer paid half. But look at it this way: If you know about that up front, you can price your services accordingly.

The other thing you will want to do regarding taxes, right at the start, is apply for an Employee Identification Number (EIN). You will need this for reporting payroll taxes if you have employees. If you set up wholesale accounts, you will also need it in order to be charged for the wholesale rate, rather than the retail rate, for any items you buy to sell to your customers.

Taxes on Product Sales

While many event planners simply buy items for their clients using the client's credit or by receiving cash up front, a few buy the items wholesale and then resell them at retail to their customers.

In most jurisdictions, if you buy items or services at wholesale prices and then resell them to your clients for a higher price, you will need to collect sales tax and turn it over to the appropriate city, county, state, and/or country. In order to collect sales tax, you must have a resale number. Also known as a tax number, a resale permit, or a sales tax permit, you are required to show this number on a certificate when you want to shop wholesale. You will not pay sales tax at the point of purchase, but will file your purchases with the state or county and mail them a check.

This application should also be available at the Occupational License Office, but you will register it with either the county or the state, depending on where you live. Again, you will have to fill out a short form with information about the nature of your business. There is usually no charge to register, and the certificate will be mailed to you within a few weeks.

Either quarterly or monthly, you will fill out a form that lists the total retail dollar amount (not wholesale amount) of the merchandise you purchased during the relevant period of time, calculate the tax owed, and mail in a check. File these forms on time, or you risk being assessed some hefty fines and interest on the amount owing.

It is very important to note that the tax is on the resale value, not the wholesale price. When you shop for wholesale items, you will want to make a habit of noting the retail price. If there is no retail price listed where you purchase the item, you can assume to double the wholesale price to get the retail.

In turn, you will also collect the sales tax from your clients, so you won't be out the money unless you sell to your clients at a marked down price. In some states and provinces you will also be eligible for a vendor's compensation (commission), which means that you can keep a very small percentage of the tax you collect as payment for being a "government agent".

When you purchase items wholesale, you may also be asked to fill out a blanket certificate of resale by the seller. This simply means that you understand the situation and agree to pay the sales tax on the items you purchase.

In Canada, the process is quite similar. You will want to contact your provincial Department of Finance to apply for a vendor's license or permit for the purpose of collecting provincial sales tax (applicable in most provinces). Also, businesses with revenue exceeding $30,000 must register with the Canada Customs and Revenue Agency for a business number in order to collect the Goods and Services Tax.

If you are able to do business entirely by using your clients' credit accounts, or if they reimburse you for anything you buy for them, you may not need a sales tax license. However, your services may be taxable, and you'll have to collect taxes on those fees and turn them over to the appropriate agency. To find out which taxes apply in your jurisdiction, check the resources at the end of this section and consult with an accountant.

Some business owners erroneously think that they can avoid paying sales tax on office supplies and other items they use within their businesses. That is not so; a business pays sales tax on anything it uses except those things they directly resell. If you were reselling paper –

for instance, if a client asked you to get him 5,000 reams of printer paper – then you would buy it at wholesale without paying sales tax and you would collect that tax from your client, who is buying it from you at retail. If you bought one ream of chartreuse paper and intended to use it for your own solicitation letters – even though you were using it to run your business – you would still pay sales tax for it. You can take a look at the rules at your own state's website.

Resources

For tax information, forms and publications, see the resources at the start of this chapter or contact your government tax authority. Check your local phone directory for an office near you, call their national office, or visit their website.

The U.S. Internal Revenue Service (IRS) can be reached at 1-800-424-3676 or online at **www.irs.gov**. In Canada, you can get information from the Canada Customs and Revenue Agency at 1-800-959-2221 or online at **www.ccra-adrc.gc.ca/tax/business**.

5.4.4 Setting Your Fees

Long before your first phone call from a prospective client you need to decide how much you will charge for your time and expertise. The most common ways for event planners to charge for their services are: Cost-Plus, Hourly Fee, and Flat Fee.

Cost-Plus

This method (also known as a percentage fee) involves charging clients a fee based on the cost of the event. Many event planners use this method, alone or in combination with an hourly fee.

After adding up all the costs of the event (before taxes), you would charge an additional 10 to 25 percent as your fee (the average is about 15 percent). So if the event costs $10,000 and your fee is 15% of the cost, you would earn $1,500. If you decide to price your services this way, determining the budget will be an important first step to ensure you can provide the service for that amount of money.

In some cases, particularly social events, this method alone may not pay enough. For example, if you are planning a children's birthday party with a budget of $500, a fee of $50 or so may not properly compensate you for your time. In such cases, we know of an event planner who charges up to 40 percent of the total cost.

If you are considering charging a percentage of the fee, keep in mind that a number of clients do not like this method. Hospitality Networks advises:

> "Select a planner who charges by the hour rather than based on a percentage of the total bill. When the planner's fee is based on a percentage of the bill there is little incentive to save you money on the cost of your event."

Hourly Fee

An hourly fee is another common way for event planners to charge for their services. Hourly rates vary widely. An experienced event planner may charge $150 per hour, while a beginner may charge $25 per hour. $50 per hour is typical.

You do not have to start at $25 per hour. In fact, you may want to charge a higher fee (such as $40 to $50 per hour) when you start because it may actually make some clients more likely to work with you. Many believe "you get what you pay for" so they may assume an event planner who charges $50 per hour is more experienced or will do a better job than one who charges $25 per hour.

Flat Fee

A flat fee (also known as a "project fee") may be used when the event is large. In some cases you may have a client that has a firm figure that the event is not to exceed, and the fee is built into the budget right from the onset. Many clients prefer this method because there are no surprises to the client (as could happen with an hourly rate) or to you.

Flat fees can range from $75 for a one-time consultation (see below) to thousands of dollars for full-service event planning. If you choose this method, be careful when estimating the time you feel it will take you to accomplish the tasks necessary for each event.

The more experience you acquire, the easier it will be to determine a flat fee for a particular job. Until you have the experience to be able to estimate how long a particular event will take you, it may be better for you to charge an hourly fee. Here are two types of flat fees that may be easier for you to determine:

Consultation Fee

Some event planners give a half-hour to one-hour free initial consultation. In such cases, this first meeting is simply an opportunity to explain how your services can benefit the client. However, other planners start charging from the first meeting.

For clients who want to do everything themselves – but want to know how to do it as easily and cost-effectively as possible – you can offer brief consultations to help them get started. For example, you might offer an hourly consultation (most planners suggest a two-hour minimum) to help them plan a schedule, recommend specific vendors, prepare a preliminary budget, and answer any questions they may have. Fees for a one-time consultation may be around $75 - $150.

If you are asked to prepare a proposal, consider charging a consultation fee, such as $150. This fee could be applied towards the event if the client decides to hire you.

On-Site Event Management Fee

One type of flat fee that is easier to determine is a day of event fee (or daily on-site fee). In this case you would handle on-site supervision and crisis management on the day of the event only. Fees for this service typically start at $500 as you may be working from early in the morning until late in the evening. Experienced event planners who need to have other staff from their company at the event, may charge a daily event coordination fee as high as $2,500 per day.

Other Options

Per Person Fee

Although not as commonly used, a per person fee arrangement is an option, particularly when planning a smaller event such as a dinner party. In this case, the event planner may charge a fee of $10 to $40 per person depending on what services are needed and how many people are attending.

If you charge a per person fee, make sure you set a minimum that will adequately compensate you for your time. The number of actual guests may be lower than the initial estimate. If the host tells you the event will involve 25 people, but only 10 decide to attend, you want to ensure your fee does not suffer as a result.

Commission

A few event planners offer their services free of charge to clients. They earn their money from commissions paid by vendors. The percentage of commission will depend on how effective a negotiator you are. Most suppliers will give you 10 percent off simply because you request a discount. (Discounts are usually passed along to the client.) If you have established a relationship with a vendor, they may offer you a higher percentage for referring business to them.

Receiving this type of "kickback" is viewed as unethical by many event planners, although it is standard practice in other industries. (For example, travel agents traditionally offered their services free of charge to travelers because they were paid a commission by airlines, hotels, and other travel suppliers.)

When deciding whether to go this route with your business, consider that some clients (those who believe "you get what you pay for") may be skeptical of an event planner who charges no fee for their service, unless they are employed by a vendor such as a hotel.

Reselling Products

As mentioned in the section on taxes, some event planners buy products (e.g. party favors) at wholesale prices and then resell them at retail to their clients. If you plan to become a reseller, make sure you review the information in section 5.4.3 on taxes.

Fundraisers

If you want to work with non-profit organizations, you may hear that they have "no money" to pay an event planner. One way to overcome that is to offer to organize a fundraising event, which could raise money for the organization and pay your fee. You might share the "gate" (money raised from ticket sales or admission fees) 50-50, or work out some other arrangement.

Some event planners make similar arrangements with sponsorships or donations that they arrange for non-profit organizations. This is a risky way to get paid, so make sure it is a cause you believe in.

Combination

Some event planners charge a combination of fees. For example, a corporate meeting planner might charge the client a flat fee combined with a percentage of the cost of the event, while a planner who does small social events might charge a flat fee plus earn a commission from vendors.

Once you have been planning events for a while, you may decide to revise your fees, or charge amounts based on different methods. With more experience or education, you may also want to raise your fees.

When setting your fees, consider the services you will provide, your experience, and what the local competition is charging. You should also determine what your overhead and administration costs are and ensure you include a portion of your costs in your fees for every event.

5.4.5 Getting Paid

Whatever type or combination of fees you decide is best for your company to offer, make sure you and your client agree to it in writing. A sample contract appears in the next section, but you will need to revise it according to the specifics of your arrangement with your client.

Deposit

It is normal for event planners to be paid a deposit (also known as a retainer) to begin the work. At the end of your initial consultation, or once the client decides to hire you, you can ask for a non-refundable deposit, such as 50% of your fee, with the balance payable on the event day. (The client will bring a check to the event.)

Paying Vendors

Many vendors will expect to be paid at the time they supply the product or service. Vendors that supply services at the time of the event (such as music or catering) can be paid at the event.

However, in some cases, these vendors will expect a deposit (e.g. 50%) to book the date. Other vendors may have to be paid in full before the event. For example, if you buy party favors from a retail store, they will likely expect you to pay when you make the purchase.

Some event planners pay all costs upfront out of the deposit (or on their credit cards), then invoice the client. To avoid risking your own funds, you have a couple of options. One option, if you are purchasing for a major corporation that has good credit, is to have the vendor supply the product and invoice the client directly. (Make sure you arrange this in advance with the client, so the invoice will be paid.) Another option is to get a check from your client so you can pay the vendor when you pick up the products or book the services.

Invoicing

The client may ask you to bring an invoice to the event (to exchange for your check). Or you may need to invoice the client after the event for any incidental expenses that you were billed for after the event. (However, many event planners do not charge for normal business expenses such as long distance telephone, office supplies, or photo-copies. Those costs are built into their fee.)

Corporate clients are usually invoiced at the end of each project, or they can be invoiced monthly if a project is ongoing. (For example, if you are planning a series of events.) A challenge with invoicing on a monthly basis is that corporations normally expect at least 30 days to pay, and some wait 60 or 90 days before putting a check in the mail.

Your invoice should be on your letterhead and include the following (see the next page for a sample).

- The client name and contact information

- The date of the invoice

- A purchase order number (if the client gave you one)

- Services you provided

- Any taxes payable

- Any expenses you have paid (also known as disbursements)

- The total amount due

- Terms of payment (e.g. "Payable upon receipt" or "Payable within 30 days")

Sample Invoice

(On Your Letterhead)

INVOICE

DATE: November 5, 2004

TO: Carla Client
       Public Relations Department
       XYZ Corporation
       123 Main Street
       Sunnyday, CA 90211

RE: Event Planning Services for November 5 Open House

       Project Fee (as per contract of Sept. 7, 2004) $2,000.00

       Tax on Project Fee *(insert your own tax rate)*   200.00

       Expenses (receipts enclosed)   195.23

                    Supplies for information kits $146.44
                    Gift for Mayor $48.79

       TOTAL   2,395.23

       Less: Deposit   (1,000.00)

       Total – Please pay this amount   **$1,395.23**

       Terms: Payable upon receipt.
       Thank you for your business.

5.5 Client Contracts

A contract is vital. It helps avoid misunderstandings and can protect you. For example, if the person who hired you leaves the company, and is replaced by someone who decides your services are no longer needed, having a contract in place can help you get paid.

Your contract can include the following:

- Your name, company name, address and contact information

- The client's name(s), address and contact information

- The date(s) and title of the event

- The location of the event

- Description of the service(s) being provided

- Any service(s) not being provided

- Fees, including payment terms, deposits, and reimbursement of expenses

- Clause outlining who is responsible for paying suppliers (you or the client)

- Cancellation policy

- Signature lines for you and the client

On the pages that follow you will find two samples. The first is a sample "engagement letter" you might use with an individual client. You could ask your clients to sign it at your initial meeting, or have them return it to you later.

The second is a services agreement which you could adapt for use with a corporate client. It covers a number of additional areas, such as a product/service liability disclaimer so that you cannot be held responsible for defects in items you buy or services you subcontract for your clients.

You can adapt these contracts to fit your needs. Before using any contract, make sure you have it reviewed by your lawyer.

Sample Engagement Letter

(On Your Letterhead)

[Insert name of Client]

[Insert address of Client]

[Date]

Dear **[Name of client]**,

As promised, I have set out below a description of the services that **[your name/company]** will provide to you.

I will provide the following services:
[Insert description of the services, such as consultations with the client, getting bids from vendors, on-site coordination of the event, etc.]

My fee for the services performed will be as follows:
[Insert rates, amount of deposit, etc.]

If you agree that the foregoing fairly sets out your understanding of our agreement, please sign a copy of this letter in the space indicated below, and return it to me at **[insert address, fax number or e-mail address]**.

Yours sincerely,

[Name]

Agreed and Accepted:

_____
[Insert name of client]

_____
Date

Sample Services Agreement

THIS AGREEMENT is made this **[date]** day of **[month]**, 200___.

BETWEEN
[insert name of your client] (the "Client"); and **[insert your name or your company's name]** (the "Event Planner"), collectively referred to as the "Parties."

The Client wishes to be provided with the Services (defined below) by the Event Planner and the Event Planner agrees to provide the Services to the Client on the terms and conditions of this Agreement.

1.1 Services

The Event Planner shall provide the following services ("Services") to the Client in accordance with the terms and conditions of this Agreement: **[Insert a description of the services here]**

1.2 Fees

As consideration for the provision of the Services by the Event Planner, the fees for the provision of the Services is **[insert fees here]** ("Fees").

The Client **[shall/shall not]** pay for the Event Planner's out-of-pocket expenses comprising **[insert here, if agreed]**.

1.3 Payment

The Client agrees to pay the Fees to the Event Planner on the following dates: **[also specify whether the price will be paid in one payment, in installments or upon completion of specific milestones]**.

The Event Planner shall invoice the Client for the Services that it has provided to the Client **[monthly/at the event/after the event]**. The Client shall pay such invoices **[upon receipt /within 30 days of receipt]** from the Event Planner.

Any charges payable under this Agreement are exclusive of any applicable taxes and such shall be payable by the Client to the Event Planner in addition to all other charges payable hereunder.

1.4 Warranty

The Event Planner represents and warrants that it will perform the Services with reasonable skill and care.

1.5 Limitation of Liability

Subject to the Client's obligation to pay the Fees to the Event Planner, either party's liability arising directly out of its obligations under this Agreement and every applicable part of it shall be limited in aggregate to the Fees.

The Event Planner assumes no liability due to the quality of items or services purchased for the Client.

1.6 Term and Termination

This Agreement shall be effective on the date hereof and shall continue until the date of the event unless terminated sooner. If the Client terminates this agreement for any reason more than 10 days before the scheduled event, the Client will forfeit the deposit paid to the Event Planner, and the Client shall reimburse the Event Planner for all outstanding out-of-pocket expenses. If the Client terminates this agreement for any reason within 10 days of the scheduled event, the full fee is payable to the Event Planner, and the Client shall reimburse the Event Planner for all outstanding out-of-pocket expenses.

1.7 Relationship of the Parties

The Parties acknowledge and agree that the Services performed by the Event Planner, its employees, sub-contractors, or agents shall be as an independent contractor and that nothing in this Agreement shall be deemed to constitute a partnership, joint venture, or otherwise between the parties.

1.8 Confidentiality

Neither Party will disclose any information of the other which comes into its possession under or in relation to this Agreement and which is of a confidential nature.

1.9 Miscellaneous

The failure of either party to enforce its rights under this Agreement at any time for any period shall not be construed as a waiver of such rights.

If any part, term or provision of this Agreement is held to be illegal or unenforceable neither the validity or enforceability of the remainder of this Agreement shall be affected.

This Agreement constitutes the entire understanding between the Parties relating to the event and supersedes all prior representations, negotiations or understandings with respect to the event.

Neither Party shall be liable for failure to perform any obligation under this Agreement if the failure is caused by any circumstances beyond its reasonable control, including but not limited to acts of god, war, or industrial dispute.

This Agreement shall be governed by the laws of the jurisdiction in which the Client is located.

Agreed by the Parties hereto:

SIGNED by _____

on behalf of_____
[the Client]

SIGNED by _____

on behalf of_____
[the Event Planner]

6. Getting Clients

"I had such a great time at the society's fundraising ball, and the dinner was amazing! How did you do it? I'm trying to plan our company's annual awards dinner, and I can't believe all the things that have to be handled."

"My event planner is _____. I'm very happy with the job she did. Would you like her telephone number?"

This is an example of the way many event planners find clients — through word of mouth. As you probably know from personal experience, a recommendation from a friend is perhaps the most powerful form of advertising that exists.

But don't despair if you are just starting out. In this section of the guide you will find a variety of ideas to help you attract clients. And once you have done a great job for those first few clients, you can start attracting more through word of mouth.

6.1 Choose Your Target Markets

Before you start trying to sell your services to prospective clients, you should decide which types of clients you want to plan events for. These are your "target" markets.

It can be tempting for a new event planner to say something like "I want to work for anyone who'll pay me!" Avoid the temptation. It is costly and time-consuming to try to market your business to "everyone" and the truth is that some people will be more interested than others in the services you have to offer. In fact, people are more likely to hire you if they see you as an "expert" who specializes in what they need.

When you are just starting out, of course you might take whatever business comes your way. However, you can focus your marketing efforts on the target markets you most want to work with. Once you start getting more business, you may be able to give up work you find less rewarding, and spend your time on clients and projects you find most rewarding.

Your target market will depend on any specialization you identified in section 5.1.1, such as meeting planning, special events, social events, destination management, etc. For example, if you want to plan special events, you might market to non-profit organizations or municipal governments.

If you want to plan meetings, you might focus your marketing efforts on large corporations, companies in a specific industry, or professional associations.

Even if you plan to offer full-service event planning, beginning with a specific market in mind can help you develop an effective marketing plan.

For example, you might decide to focus on marketing your services to private clubs such as country clubs, golf clubs, faculty clubs, and yacht clubs. You could develop marketing materials specifically aimed at people who want to organize events at private clubs, and you could concentrate on developing relationships with the general managers of those clubs.

See the story on the next page of one event planner who developed a business by partnering with another company.

This is also true for social events. For example, if you want to plan children's birthday parties, joining the Chamber of Commerce may not be as cost-effective for you as it would be for someone who wants to plan social events (such as dinner parties, holiday parties, etc.) for executives.

Once you have decided who your target markets are, you can prepare materials and plan marketing activities that will most appeal to those groups.

As you get more experience you may decide to go after new target markets, or your business may naturally evolve to focus on particular types of clients. However, starting with some specific target markets in mind can help you focus your marketing efforts most efficiently – saving you both time and money.

Partnering with Another Company

Lynn Simpson, now a self-employed event planner in Carlsbad, California, remembers how she first got into the business:

I was working as a Jill of All Trades for a company that rents out boats as part of their floating bed and breakfast business. I scrubbed boats, cleaned rooms, crewed on the cruises, checked people in and took reservations. Occasionally, the guests coming aboard would be spending the night for a special occasion – an anniversary, birthday, something like that. I started putting special packages together for them and adding special personalized touches.

Once a young man called to arrange a stay with a cruise in order to propose to his girlfriend. He was so sweet and wanted everything to be perfect — money was no object. I took on arranging the details to make it a Cinderella moment. I bought dozens of flowers (yellow roses — her favorite), iced their favorite brand of champagne, loaded the CD player with all their favorite songs, created a menu (all her favorite foods) with a local caterer, and went to the local chocolatier to have a special dessert created for them. Everything turned out to be magical — she said "yes" and I decided right then I wanted to arrange special events for many more people.

In the months to come, the charter/bed and breakfast company decided to buy the deli at the marina where their boats were moored. I became a "working partner" and started to do catering for local businesses and other charter companies.

Before long, I was taking on event planning jobs for all sorts of people — from intimate dinner cruises to corporate functions. It may have been an unusual way of creating my own event planning business, but I love the work and am happy to have found a way to start my own business.

Like Lynn, you may find a steady source of clients by partnering with another successful business. It might be a private club, an attraction – even a charter boat company!

6.2 Promotional Tools

The promotional tools that can help market your business begin with your business card, but may also include a brochure, portfolio, and website.

6.2.1 Brochures

You will have many opportunities to give out your business card. In fact, you should get in the habit of giving it to almost everyone you meet. But there are also times to give out brochures. For example, when you give a presentation at a networking meeting (see section 6.3.1) or when people seem particularly interested in your services. You should also provide some to the companies with whom you do a lot of business. Your major vendors should have some, in case someone asks them if they know an event planner they could recommend.

Your brochure will contain your company name and contact information, including your web address. It can also include some of the information you have on your website, such as:

- Photographs of events you have planned

- Benefits of hiring an event planner (e.g. save time, enjoy a stress-free event)

- A list of the services you provide

- A photograph of you

- Some testimonials from satisfied customers

Your brochure can be folded in three, with printing on both sides of the sheet, or you can simply print a one-page flyer which you could also pin up on bulletin boards. If you are printing only a few copies of your brochure, you may be able to find nice paper at your local office supply store which you can run through your PC's printer.

If you aren't able to produce brochures on your home computer, or if you need hundreds of brochures (for example, if you are participating in a trade show), it may be faster and cheaper for you to have your brochures professionally printed. Check the Yellow Pages under "Printers," or use the printing services of your local office supply store.

> TIP: Be sure you spell-check and grammar check every-
>   thing. Also check your phone number, e-mail address,
>   and other contact information carefully to make sure
>   clients can reach you.

When you decide you do need professionally printed brochures, check the Yellow Pages under "Printers" or use quick-printer services such as Kinko's or Minuteman Press or even the printing services of your local office supply store.

6.2.2 Your Portfolio

A portfolio shows examples of your work and may include the following items from events you have planned, or been involved with:

- photographs of the event

- collateral materials from the event (e.g. flyers, brochures, post-ers, news releases, etc.)

- testimonial letters from companies or organizations that you planned the events for

- letters, notes or copies of e-mails from attendees congratulat-ing you on the success of the event

- newspaper clippings of the event

- anything else that shows your skill as an event planner

A portfolio offers a prospective customer proof that you have the skills and creativity to do the job. Read on to find out how to get items for your portfolio and how to put it together. At the end of this section you'll find some tips on how to create a portfolio if you don't yet have materials from actual events.

Photographs

They say a picture says a thousand words, and nowhere is this more true than when you are trying to sell yourself as being creative, imagi-native and organized.

As mentioned in Chapter 3, try to arrange to get photographs from every event you work on. In fact, with the first few events you plan for friends or relatives, you might offer your event planning services for free in exchange for photographs to put into your portfolio. While you won't include every photograph in your portfolio, it is a good idea to have as many photos as possible to choose from.

When selecting photographs, remember that your portfolio should be a collection of your best examples, ideally showing happy people. Most clients do not have time to look through hundreds of photographs, so be selective about what to include.

One suggested guideline is to choose 15-20 photographs of work you are really proud of (if you have that many different photos). It's ideal if you have planned several different types of events, so you can show some variety. If not, simply use what you have.

Letters of Recommendation

The best letters of recommendation are those written by clients you have done event planning work for. However, you can also include letters of recommendation from past employers if the letters say good things about your abilities in areas that are important in the event planning business, such as interpersonal skills and organizational ability. You can also include appropriate thank you notes you have received.

As was emphasized in Chapter 3, every time you plan an event for someone — even a friend or family member (preferably with a different last name from yours!) — ask for a letter of recommendation. When you ask for a letter, keep in mind that many people are busy so they are more likely to do what you ask if you can make it as easy as possible.

To help get the kind of recommendation letter you want, and make the job easier on the person writing the letter, you could supply a list of points they might mention. For example, you could mention:

- what you did (write it out for them — chances are you remember exactly what you did more clearly than they might)

- how you saved them money by finding the best vendors

- how you got along well with everyone you worked with

- how you came up with many creative ideas

- how you handled every detail so well they didn't have to worry about a thing

- that everyone has commented on how beautiful the event was

Of course, all these things don't have to be included in a single letter! The specifics will depend on the particular job you did, but even a few glowing sentences can help you look good to customers.

If you feel your relative or friend will not write a great letter – even if you specifically suggest what to include – you can offer to compose the letter yourself and have them simply supply the signature. You should have a couple of different letters written specifically for this purpose and propose one of them as an alternative. Here is a sample reference letter:

Sample Reference Letter

Dear Evan Event Planner,

On behalf of the entire organization, I would like to take this opportunity to thank you again for the wonderful job you did on planning our big event! It was perfect and exactly what we had always hoped it would be.

Your ideas and creative touches made our event unique and one we will not soon forget. You promised total organization, and that is exactly what you delivered. What you didn't tell us was what a pleasure it would be to work with you. Your calming demeanor helped extinguish all the little fires that crop up, and for that we are thankful.

We will certainly recommend your service to our associates, and wish you success in the years to come.

Sincerely,
Vicky Vice President

TIP: A recommendation letter should preferably not mention that you worked for free. You want to give the impression that your work has value, and a customer may assume the reason you received such a glowing recommendation is because you didn't charge anything. Remember, good work is good work no matter how much you were paid for it.

What Else to Include

Your portfolio can include anything else that could impress someone who is considering hiring you. For example, if you have a certificate of membership in an event planning association or for completion of an event planning course, put the actual certificate in your portfolio. If that's not possible, include a photocopy or a photograph of the certificate.

Likewise, if your event planning business has been mentioned in a newspaper or magazine story, you could include a clipping or photocopy of the published article. Later in this chapter, you will find information about how to write articles for publication, and other ways to establish your reputation as an event planning expert.

Some event planners also include sample event timelines or other planning materials in their portfolios.

Putting It All Together

There are several different options for displaying the materials in your portfolio. One possibility is to put everything into a professional looking three-ring binder with plastic sheet covers to protect the pages. If you wish, you can mount your photographs and other portfolio materials onto thin cardboard. All of these supplies are available from any office supplies store.

Another possibility is to use a portfolio case, which you can buy at an art supply store (check the Yellow Pages). Portfolio or presentation cases comes in a variety of sizes (e.g. 11" x 14", 14" x 17", 17" x 22") and cost from about $15 to over $150, depending on the size, material, and how fancy you want it to be. However, customers are interested in what is inside the case, so you don't need to spend a lot of money on the case itself (e.g. you could get vinyl instead of leather).

The following websites have some examples: **www.dickblick.com** (do a search for portfolio) and **www.keysan.com//ksu0601.htm**.

Another option is to have a series of folders marked with the date, name and type of event and who you set up the event for. Include these folders in a master folder (or portfolio case) so you can keep all your details together.

How to Create a Portfolio without Experience

If you don't yet have materials from actual events you have organized, you can create materials. For example, you could come up with an idea for an event, then produce a collage of what you would do for that event. Include magazine photos of food, design a sample invitation (check a local stationery store for ideas), create an event day itinerary, etc.

If you have a camera and can take decent photos, you can also create your own photographs. For example, you could decorate your own dining room table or construct a balloon archway. As soon as you've planned an event or two, you will have pictures from an actual event and can drop the others from your portfolio.

You can use any of the methods described above to display your materials. However, it can be particularly impressive to put your samples onto picture matting or heavy poster board, which you can buy from an art supply store. (Check the Yellow Pages.) Your board can be white, black, or another color that you feel looks best with your samples. The size can be 14" x 17", 15" x 20", or any size that allows you to effectively display the materials.

You can arrange the samples on a board in a way that looks most attractive to you. While you can use glue to attach your samples, using double-sided tape can help you avoid any bumps caused by glue.

6.2.3 Your Website

A website gives prospective clients the opportunity to preview your services 24 hours a day.

If you've never developed a website before – and relatively few people have – you won't have to spend a lot to do the job well. You may already have Microsoft Front Page or Netscape Composer (which comes free with the Netscape browser) installed on your computer. Both of those are relatively simple to use to create an attractive website.

But then you have to upload (send) the files to a server. The good news is that you don't have to be a computer genius to do this. You can use one of the many full-service companies that register your domain name (i.e. a name such as paulaplanner.com), host your website for a small monthly fee and submit it to search engines so clients can find you. They include Yahoo at **http://webhosting.yahoo .com** and Network Solutions at **www.netsol.com**.

You can find out about other, similar companies by visiting Webhost Magazine's website at **www.webhostmagazine.com**. Webhost Magazine offers free, unbiased consumer reports on domain name registrars and web hosting companies. It also has a tutorial guide you can use to educate yourself about everything you need to know when it comes to the Internet and setting up a website.

> **TIP:** Avoid using free web hosting sites. They will bombard visitors to your site with pop-up ads that can turn off prospective clients.

Here are a few tips for creating your website. To get additional ideas for your website, visit those of other event planners by doing an Internet search for Event Planners.

- Do include all the information your brochure contains, and consider adding some photos from your portfolio. To explain what is in the photos, you could include captions, or details such as the location, guests, entertainment, menu, decor, etc.

- Mention if you offer a free consultation and be sure you ask people to take action (e.g. "Call today").

- A nice addition is an "About Us" section, in which you can describe your experience, your philosophy and anything else you think will make your service attractive to clients.

- Add any additional information that you think will help sell your services (e.g. benefits of hiring an event planner, event planning tips you have written).

- Be sure it contains your contact information: e-mail address, phone and fax numbers, and your "snailmail" address (if you don't want people to show up at your home office without an appointment, get a post office box).

- Do make it visually attractive. Clients will judge your taste and style by what they see on your site. If necessary, consider hiring a professional web designer.

Whenever you publish photos of your clients – on your website or in print – be sure you have them sign a model release form, which gives you permission to use the images in any of your promotional materials without remuneration. Most people are happy to have their image used in such a positive way, but there may be exceptions. Asking gives them the opportunity to say they'd rather not participate, which is fine. People are entitled to their privacy, and you'll find lots of others who'd like to help.

Here is a sample of a model release form you can use:

Sample Model Release Form

I hereby give (insert your name) permission to use my photograph taken of me on (insert date) at (insert location) for promotional, online or commercial purposes. I am of legal age.

_____
(Print Name)

_____
(Signature)

_____
(Date)

Should You Link to Vendors on Your Website?

Some vendors are happy to have you link to them on your website, and some event planners feel it adds credibility to their website to show they work with reputable vendors. However, this may actually result in less business for you — your expertise is in rounding up exactly what your clients want so they won't have to. You don't want them to organize the event by themselves, do you?

You want people to call you and make appointments, not just work through your website. If they see another company's logo and a link on your website, they may think that you are promoting that company's goods over others, or that your salary comes from them.

While it's okay to mention venues in the photos you include (for example: *Gala Dinner at the Yacht Club*) you should avoid linking to specific venues or vendors.

Once you have created your website you want people to find it. Make sure you include your web address on your card and your brochure. You can even add it to your voice-mail message.

If you want new clients to find you, one way to get on the search engines is to go directly to each one and look for a link to submit your site. For example, if you go to Yahoo.com, at the bottom of the page you will find a link that says "How to suggest a site." You can find others at **http://searchenginewatch.com**. Your web hosting company may offer a search engine submission service for an extra fee.

6.3 Marketing Techniques

6.3.1 Networking Opportunities

There are different definitions of networking, but a particularly useful definition is the one given in the *American Heritage Dictionary of the English Language*:

"To interact or engage in informal communication with others for mutual assistance or support."

As you will see from this definition, two keys to networking are that it is "informal" and "mutual." This type of networking includes meeting and interacting with people informally at social and business events. This is where it really pays to have clearly defined your target markets. You simply do not have the time to network with "everyone" who might possibly ever have a need for an event planner.

While some of the people you meet may have an immediate need for an event planner (or know someone who does), in many cases you are laying the foundation for future business. By establishing relationships through networking, you can be the one people think of when they need an event planner.

This section offers a variety of ideas, but you don't have to do all of them. Choose a few to begin with, based on your target markets. If the first ones you try don't turn out to be great networking opportunities, scratch them off your list and try something else.

Meeting with Vendors

Earlier in this guide you were given advice on developing relationships with vendors, with the aim of learning about event planning and finding resources to recommend to your clients. Another very important reason to develop relationships with vendors is so they can refer business to you.

> **TIP:** Referrals from vendors is an incredible source of potential revenue that many event planners overlook. Consider establishing relationships with vendors. They could bring you a steady stream of new clients without advertising!

Arrange meetings with as many vendors as possible —— venues, caterers, florists, rental companies, photographers, etc. Remember, you are not only there to get to know what products and services each vendor supplies, but to give them the chance to get to know you.

Bring business cards and brochures and prepare to sell yourself and your event planning services. Tell the person you are speaking with that you believe in mutually rewarding relationships and would be pleased to send your clients to them. In turn, you would appreciate it if they would pass on your name to their prospective clients that have not contracted an event planner.

As was mentioned earlier, it is extremely important for you to foster a good working relationship with many vendors. It is true that people do business with those they like and respect, and if they like and respect you, they will recommend you. Following the tips in the sections on working with vendors and developing interpersonal communication skills can help you build a great network.

Attending Trade Shows

Conventions for the hospitality industry can be a great place to connect with vendors and find associates who may need some help. You can find out about upcoming events through your local Convention & Visitors Bureau, or do a search for upcoming events at the Trade Show Exhibitors Association website at **www.tsea.org**.

Bridal shows are also a great source: caterers, florists, restaurants and facility owners may be looking for event planners to help during peak months. Besides, a visit to these shows is a great time to build your Rolodex with potential vendors for upcoming projects and can provide you with inspiration for your next event.

Networking Clubs

A valuable form of networking is through a networking club. Some of these are general business groups, but many have a target group of clients and include one member from different industries (e.g. insurance, financial planning, law, professional photography, real estate, etc.) to reach those in the target group. Each member of the club is expected to bring a certain number of leads to the group each week or month.

Fees will vary but can be as low as the cost of breakfast once a week or breakfast plus a membership fee. You may also be required to serve on the executive board after a time. In addition to the marketing opportunities, benefits of joining networking groups may include discounts on services provided by other members of the group.

To become a member you are either recommended to the group by an existing member, or you might approach the group and ask to sit in as an observer for a meeting or two, and get accepted from there. Most groups will allow a trial period before demanding that you join or stop coming to meetings. You may be asked to give a short presentation about your own business, and on what business and personal skills you can bring to the group.

The types of participants will differ with every group, so don't settle for the first one you visit. Check around first before deciding which one to join. Make sure the members represent the kind of very busy people with reasonable incomes who might become clients for you, or who would know others who could benefit from your services.

One way to find a networking club is through word of mouth. Ask individuals in sales jobs — such as insurance agents, financial planners, computer sales professionals, car salesmen, travel agents.

You can also look for networking groups online. Business Network International has more than 2,300 chapters in cities around the world. Their website is **www.bni.com**.

Membership Organizations

Another excellent way to network is by joining associations that prospective clients may belong to. Some examples include:

- Civic and service clubs (such as Rotary Club or Kiwanis Club)

- Business organizations (such as your Chamber of Commerce)

- Clubs that attract the wealthy (for example, golf, polo, yachting, and country clubs)

Membership fees may vary from $20 to hundreds or even thousands of dollars (the latter if you want to join an exclusive country club or private golf club). The more expensive clubs usually require current members to introduce you and put you up for membership, so you may have to join some less exclusive clubs in order to meet people who might also belong to the more expensive clubs. Many less exclusive clubs will let you attend a few times for a nominal fee so you can decide if you really want to join.

You can find organizations by asking your friends and colleagues what they are involved in. You can also find them in your local telephone directory or online. Here are a couple to get you started:

- *Executive Women International*
  Phone: 801-355-2800
  Fax: 801-355-2852
  Email: ewi@executivewomen.org
  www.executivewomen.org

- *World Chamber of Commerce Directory*
  Telephone: 970-663-3231
  Fax: 970-663-6187
  www.chamberofcommerce.com

If you simply attend club functions without getting involved, the value of the membership will not be as great as if you truly pitch in.

What sorts of things can you do to help out and gain the attention of others whose goodwill can help your business grow? Here are some suggestions:

- Serve on a committee

- Write articles for the association newsletter

- Volunteer to help out with the organization's events

- Run for election to the Executive Committee

Here are some additional networking tips specifically for meeting wealthy people.

Attend Openings

When a museum or art gallery has a new exhibit, they will hold an "opening" which may attract a crowd of wealthy and cultured people – exactly the type of people who could use your services. An opening usually combines a social event, such as a wine and cheese reception, with an opportunity for people to view the exhibit. For the museum or gallery, these events can be an excellent opportunity to make sales, attract donations, or simply get the word out about their new exhibit. Some museums and galleries hold several openings throughout the year.

There is usually no cost or obligation to attend. In some cases, getting invited to these events can be as simple as phoning and asking to be put on the mailing list. Another possibility is to visit local art galleries that are also dealers (retailers) and speak with the owner or manager. Ask to be put on their mailing list and notified of upcoming events.

Get Involved with Charities

Many wealthy and professional people attend charitable fundraising events such as fashion shows, teas, luncheons, dinners, etc. Attending these events yourself is one way to start connecting with the wealthy, but it can be very expensive. (Since they are "fundraisers", getting into each event might cost you $100 or more!) Plus, there may not be much time to meet and mingle with other attendees.

You will have a much greater opportunity to connect with people and support a good cause by volunteering to help with the event. As a volunteer you may work closely with the type of people you want to attract as clients. Many wealthy people don't just make financial donations – they also donate their time to charities, and are actively involved in fundraising and event planning.

Volunteer for activities that will bring you into contact with these people. In other words, leave the envelope stuffing to other volunteers and focus on helping organize events. In addition to serving on committees, see if you can volunteer the services of your event planning business.

This may be a wonderful opportunity not only to meet people, but to get the name of your firm in front of every person who attends the event! Most organizations publish a brochure or booklet to give to each attendee. This usually contains information about the event along with a list of suppliers – including the name of the company that supplied event planning services.

So which charities do your target markets get involved with? If you have read *Town & Country* magazine or the social column of a local newspaper, you have probably seen photos of wealthy people at charitable events. The rich typically are involved in arts organizations, including:

- ballet
- theater
- symphony
- opera
- visual arts

Many are also involved in health causes, such as organizations that work to find cures for AIDS or Breast Cancer. Others are involved with political campaigns (although technically not a "charity," political campaigns do fundraising events where you can meet prospective clients).

To volunteer, simply phone up the organizations in your community that interest you. You may be able to find them through word of mouth or listed in the Yellow Pages under a category such as "Societies" or "Charitable Organizations."

You might consider getting involved with cultural organizations, as well. Organizations formed for a single purpose, such as running your city's St. Patrick's Day Parade, are other places to find busy people who could benefit from your services.

When you choose organizations to get involved with, be sure that you have some interest in the work they do. Otherwise you will find yourself avoiding meetings and missing the chance to get involved in ways that can both help your business and carry out the mission of the organization.

6.3.2 Promotional Events

Give a Speech

Even if you don't join an organization, you may still be able to connect with their members and get new business by being a speaker at a breakfast meeting, luncheon, or workshop.

The topic can be anything related to event planning that their members would be interested in. For example, if you're speaking to a business networking group, you might talk on "How to Promote Your Services to Event Organizers," while a women's group might be interested in hearing tips on how to plan a successful social event.

While you probably will not be paid for your presentations, it can be an excellent opportunity to promote your business. Your company name may be published in the organization's newsletter, it will be mentioned by the person who introduces you, you can distribute business cards and brochures, and you will be able to mingle with attendees before and after your presentation. (You may get a free breakfast or lunch too!)

If you give a good talk and offer useful advice, you will be seen as an expert. As long as there are people in the audience who need event planning services, this can be an excellent way to attract clients. To let people know that you are available to speak, contact the local organizations mentioned above and ask friends and acquaintances if they belong to any groups that have presentations from speakers.

If you feel your speaking skills could be better, there are a couple of relatively painless ways to get comfortable talking to large groups. You can hire a speaking coach. Or you can join Toastmasters, a national organization that helps people develop their speaking skills. To find a Toastmasters chapter near you, you can check your local phone book, call their world headquarters in California at (949) 858-8255, or visit **www.toastmasters.org**.

Teach a Class

Teaching a class can be a great way to earn extra money, establish your reputation, and meet prospective clients. You don't have to have a degree to teach adults—just lots of enthusiasm and knowledge of your subject.

The first step is to review the current catalog of continuing education courses offered by local colleges, universities and other organizations that provide adult education classes in your community. Call and ask for a print catalog if they do not have course information at their website. Once you have reviewed their current list of courses, come up with some ideas for new courses. (They already have instructors for any courses that are in their catalog.)

Once you have an idea for a new course in mind, call the college or organization and ask to speak with whoever hires continuing education instructors. They will tell you what you need to do to apply to teach a course.

Your Own Workshops or Seminars

While teaching continuing education courses can be rewarding, it normally takes months for a new course to be offered (and there's always the chance the continuing education program may decide not to offer it). If you'd like to start presenting courses right away, consider designing and giving your own workshops or seminars.

You will need to choose a date and time (evenings are usually best for business people) and a location, such as a meeting room at a hotel or conference center.

You will then have to decide how much to charge (consider making the fee comparable to continuing education courses offered in your community), or it may be free if you are offering it in conjunction with a retailer.

If you are working with a retailer, they will likely market it to their customers. However, they will expect you to do some marketing yourself, and you will be responsible for getting registrations yourself if you hold it at another location. The following is from the *FabJob.com Guide to Become a Motivational Speaker* which gives detailed advice on how to market a seminar:

When preparing your marketing materials, remember to focus on communicating all the benefits of attending. As well as the information, benefits of attending a seminar may include: a fun night out, a chance to network, or personal advice from an expert. Among the other items you might include in a brochure:

- Who should attend

- When and where the seminar takes place

- The speaker's credentials

- Testimonials

- That enrollment is limited (mention if past seminars sold out)

- A call to action such as "Register now!"

- How to register, including your phone number and web address

Brochures with this information can also be used to market seminars to the public. The ideal brochure for a public seminar is one that can double as a poster (e.g. printed on one side of a colorful 8½" x 11" sheet). If permitted, try posting them at bulletin boards, especially bookstores and college campuses – two places you're likely to find people interested in seminars.

Trade Shows

If you specialize in social events you may be able to find prospective clients at public shows such as women's conferences. If you are selling to the corporate market, you might consider participating in a trade show for a particular industry.

The cost to become an exhibitor (i.e. to get a booth at the show) will vary depending on the particular show, the location, the number of people expected to attend, and the amount of space you require. It may range from as little as $50 to $1,000 or more for public shows, or up to thousands of dollars for trade shows. To cut costs, you could partner with another non-competing exhibitor and share a booth space.

However, before investing in a trade show booth, attend the event if possible, or speak to some past exhibitors. While you may find a $100 booth at a women's show is a good investment to market a party planning business, $1,000 spent on a trade show booth to promote meeting planning services could give disappointing results. (Trade shows are often used to raise awareness rather than generate immediate sales.)

You can find out about upcoming shows by contacting your local convention centers, exhibition halls, or chamber of commerce. You can search for events by industry, type of event and location at **www.tradeshows.com**. For most events, you can then click on a link to find out contact information.

Many shows now have their own websites and provide registration information as well as site maps and logistical information. When setting up your booth you should bring business cards, your company brochures, and your portfolio for display at your booth.

When you speak with prospective clients, mention a few of the ideas you have for creating a spectacular event (but don't give away too much for free). To arrange consultations and discuss possible bookings, bring an appointment book or calendar of events you already have on the books. This information is very important to know if you are a one-person operation and have already booked events to plan in the coming months.

TIP: If you don't have an assistant, find a partner or even a spouse or close friend to help out at the show. The days can be long and tiring, and you won't want to close down your booth to take breaks.

6.3.3 Advertising

While networking can be a particularly effective way to get business for your event planning company, you may also be able to attract some clients through advertising.

Yellow Pages

You have probably used the Yellow Pages many times. But before you buy an ad for your own business, you should carefully investigate the costs compared to the potential return. Many new business owners find a Yellow Pages ad does not make the phone ring off the hook with buyers. If someone does respond to your ad, they may be "shopping around," so you must be prepared to invest time as well as advertising dollars if you use this method of advertising.

To minimize your risk, you might want to consider starting with a small display ad, such as a 1/8 page ad. If you can get your hands on a previous year's edition of your local Yellow Pages, compare the ads for event planners from year to year. If you notice others have increased or decreased the size of their ads, this can give you an indication of what might work for you. Also, if you are doing information interviews, you can ask event planners how well their Yellow Pages ads are working for them.

You can either design the ad yourself, have the Yellow Pages design it for you, or hire a designer. Take a look at the ads in the events category of your current Yellow Pages for ideas. If you are interested in advertising, contact your local Yellow Pages to speak with a sales rep. Check your phone book for contact information.

Some localities also have "pages" or "books" of other types. In the mid-Atlantic states, the community Yellow Pages are alternatives. These are limited to smaller geographic areas than, for example, a whole state or city. Check into that possibility, as well, especially if you don't want to travel great distances to find clients.

Magazines

Magazine advertising can be expensive, and may not generate the results you want unless you do it repeatedly. (It has been estimated that many people need to see an advertisement three to seven times before they buy.)

If you choose to buy advertising, it will probably be most cost-effective to place ads in small local magazines or newspapers. The publications you advertise in will usually design your ad for an additional cost, and give you a copy of the ad to run in other publications. Here are some tips for effective advertising:

- Make your ad about your customers. Explain how they can benefit from your services rather than just listing the services you provide. (Saying "Your event will be the talk of the town" is better than saying "I can help you plan your next event.")

- Make them an offer they can't refuse. Your ad should describe a service or special promotion that makes you stand out from your competition. It should also include a call to action (i.e. saying "Call today" or including a coupon that expires by a certain date).

- Make sure you're available for people who respond to your ad. If someone wants to talk to you but keeps getting your voice mail, they may give up.

- Make long-term plans for your advertising program. Chances are that running an ad once won't give you as much business as you would hope. Develop a long-term advertising strategy and stick with it.

However, you will get much better results if you can get free publicity.

6.3.4 Free Media Publicity

The "media" are magazines, newspapers, radio, and television. When a business gets publicity in a magazine article, newspaper story, radio or television talk show, it can result in a tremendous amount of new business. Here are some ways event planners can get publicity:

Society Column

Many city magazines and daily newspapers in large cities have a "society" type column where they publish photos of people attending local charitable events. Every time you are involved with a charitable event, phone to invite the local publications to attend.

Because they cannot attend every event they're invited to, publications will sometimes publish photos submitted to them. So consider hiring a photographer to get some shots of you with the executive director of the charity and any celebrity special guests. Attach a label to the back of the best photo, indicating the name of the organization, event, date, and who's in the photo. Submit it immediately after the event.

Press Releases

A press release is a brief document that you submit to the media with the aim of getting publicity for your business. The ideal press release is a single page (under 500 words) and is written like a news story. You can find information on writing and submitting a press release in section 2.6.2.

Most magazines and newspapers publish contact information for their editors. Newspapers may have dozens of editors, so make sure you send your submission to the appropriate one (for example, the Lifestyle Editor). As an alternative to writing a press release, you could find out who the editor is, and either phone or send a brief "pitch" letter by email, fax or mail to suggest an idea for a story.

In your pitch, remember to focus on something that will be interesting to readers. For example, you might suggest a story on how to save money on events or unique locations to hold special events. Do some brainstorming or consider a story based on the most common kinds of questions customers ask you.

While it is not necessary to submit photographs to a daily newspaper editor (most newspapers have their own photographers), photographs may help attract the editor's attention. They might also be published in a smaller magazine, newspaper or newsletter that doesn't have a photographer on staff. If you send photos (remember to make sure you have permission from the people in the photos as well as the photographer), put them in an attractive two-pocket folder with your business card and a cover letter. Then follow up a week later with a phone call.

Write an Article or Column

One of the best ways to establish yourself as an expert is to write articles or a column for a newspaper, magazine, or newsletter. While it can be tough to break into large daily newspapers, there may be an opportunity to write for smaller newspapers or local magazines.

You could write on any topic related to planning an event, or propose an "Ask the Event Planner" column where you would answer questions from readers. The length and frequency of your column will depend on the publication. You might produce a weekly 500-word column for a local newspaper, or a monthly 1,000-word column for a newsletter or magazine.

Make sure your article or column provides valuable information to the publication's readers. As with press releases, articles that sound like an ad for your services are not likely to get published.

Once you have written your first column or article, phone the editor to ask if they would be interested in seeing it. If so, they will probably ask you to email it. If they want to publish it, they may offer to pay you. However, even if they don't pay, you should consider letting them publish it in return for including a brief bio and your contact information at the end of the article or column.

Television and Radio Talk Shows

Phone local radio and TV shows to let them know you are available to provide event planning advice to their viewers or listeners. Shows that might be appropriate include morning shows and afternoon talk shows. The person to contact is the producer of each show.

The producer will probably ask you to send them some information, so be prepared to email or fax a few paragraphs about yourself, along with a list of frequently asked questions. These are questions their audience would likely be interested in knowing the answer to. You can put any questions you like on the list, but chances are whatever you find people asking your advice about are questions that an audience would be interested in, as well.

Television is a visual medium, so it's also a good idea to invite them to come and shoot the event.

6.4 Marketing to Corporate Clients

Working with corporate clients can be fun, exciting, and financially rewarding. Many of the techniques already mentioned in this chapter can help you break into the corporate market. For example, clients may hire you after meeting you at networking events, hearing you give a speech, or reading about you in the newspaper.

However, you don't have to wait for clients to call you. Instead, you can take the initiative and contact prospective clients. In this section you will learn how to take the initiative and break into this lucrative market.

6.4.1 Your Warm Market

Your "warm market" is anyone who knows you. It includes friends, family members, neighbors, former co-workers, members of organizations you belong to, and anyone else you know. These are people that you already have a relationship with. If you phone them, you know they will return the call.

Chances are, your warm market includes a number of people who are "decision-makers" in an organization that could use your services. In other words, they are in a position where they could hire your company. If not, they may be able to recommend your services to the decision-maker. But even before getting the corporation on board as a client, you may find a number of individuals in your warm market who can use your services.

Call or send a personal letter to let family members and friends know that you have started an event planning business. If you send a letter, include a few business cards in the envelope and encourage the recipient to pass them on to everyone they know who may be planning an event in the future.

Sample Warm Market Letter

Dear Aunt Mary,

I hope this letter finds you well. Mom tells me you are planning a trip to Paris. I hope you have a wonderful time, and I'm very happy to hear you will be back in time for next summer's family reunion.

I am writing to you with some exciting news. I've decided to take my passion for everything event related and turn it into a business. Starting my own business is certainly scary and it took a big leap of faith to leave my full-time job for a part-time one but I'm sure it will be worth it.

I've been told that one of the best ways to find new clients is through word of mouth and I'm hoping you will pass my business card to anyone in your church group who is planning a party or event.

I hope you enjoy Paris and look forward to seeing you very soon.

Love,
Eva

Many event planners get their start by picking up the phone and calling people they know. However, even when contacting people you know, it's important to remember that you are calling about a business matter. While you may get the odd project purely on the basis of your relationship with someone, in most cases in order to get hired you will need to communicate the value you will bring to the company.

6.4.2 Cold Calling

Cold calling involves picking up the telephone and calling strangers. It is something many people fear doing. But it can be an effective way of generating business for those who are confident and not too afraid of hearing the word "no".

Because the reality is that some people will say "no". Some will not even give you the opportunity to say why you are calling. However, it is also a reality that there are people who need event planning services who don't know where to turn – and would welcome a call from someone who can help them.

With that in mind, look at each call as simply an introduction of your services – services that could possibly help this person and organization. Here's a short course in cold-calling that you can use no matter what corporate market you choose.

Finding Contact Information

The first step in making cold calls is to have a list of companies to call. The obvious way to get phone numbers is to pick up the Yellow Pages and choose companies in industries you'd like to work with. However, the Yellow Pages won't give you a contact name.

For more detailed information about companies in your community, you can call your local Chamber of Commerce to see if you can get a list of their members. Some chambers will only give the list to other members. In which case you may either decide to join the Chamber of Commerce (if you haven't done so already), or buy the list.

Another alternative is to find the membership list at your local public library. The central library in your city will very likely have numerous business directories, including one or more directories with contact information for local businesses. This information may be broken down by industry and company size.

Once you've decided on the companies you'd like to solicit, you'll need to identify the best person to speak with, the decision-maker. Depending on your specialization and the size of the company, there may actually be several people in the organization that could use your services. For example, any of the following departments might use the services of an event planner:

- CEO or President

- Marketing

- Public Relations

- Corporate Communications

- Human Resources

- Sales

You could call to introduce your services to decision-makers in each of these departments. (In many large organizations, the key decision-maker in each department has the title of Vice-President, Director, or Department Head. On the other hand, if the company is small, there may be a single individual you should talk to, such as an owner or office manager.

If you don't have the name of a decision-maker when you call a company, simply ask the receptionist. You might ask: "Can you tell me the name of the person who plans meetings and social events for your company?" Or you might ask: "What is the name of the Vice-President in charge of Marketing?"

When you get a name from a receptionist, make sure you ask for the correct spelling and the correct extension or direct line. If the name could belong either to a male or female (like Tracy, Chris, or Pat), also ask if the person is a man or a woman.

If you have asked who plans meetings and social events,and the re-ceptionist doesn't know, ask for the assistant to the CEO, or the mar-keting department. They are likely to know who that person is (one of them may actually be in charge of it). If the receptionist puts you through to an assistant in the decision-maker's department, you can go through the same procedure of asking for the decision-maker's name and di-rect phone number.

Be prepared, however, that the assistant may be a "gatekeeper." In other words, it may be the assistant's job to screen out calls from anyone the decision-maker doesn't know. While this certainly won't happen every time, it is something to prepare for. Remember that this person has a great deal of power over whether you ever get an ap-pointment with the decision-maker. So do not bully the assistant.

If he or she says, "Just send us your information," politely explain that while you will be happy to do that, you want to make sure the informa-tion addresses the company's needs and would like just a couple of minutes to check those out with the decision-maker. Then ask the assistant to advise you about the best time to call the decision-maker.

The sections that follow this one offer some suggested alternatives in the event that you are not able to get through to the decision-maker on the telephone. However, let's assume that you will be put through to the decision-maker. Now you need to know what to say.

What to Say

It would be great if you could just strike up a spontaneous conversa-tion with a prospective client and convince them to hire you. However, most people who are starting out don't find it easy to say the right things off the top of their head. So it's a good idea to have scripts for leaving a message on voicemail as well as for your first conversation with a potential client. A script is simply an outline of what you want to say during your call. It helps you clearly communicate the main points you want to get across.

Be prepared for the fact that many decision-makers screen their calls with voice mail. They simply don't have time to speak with everyone who wants their attention. Whether or not they return your call de-pends primarily on how intriguing your message is.

First, here's an example of what not to say:

> "Um, hi. My name is Paul Planner. I'm an event planner. Well, actually, I'm just beginning my career as an event planner, mainly for meetings because I know they're always in demand and my family really needs the money I can make from this. I've done a lot of event planning for my friends' birthday parties, and they said I was really good at it, so I thought I'd see how it works out to do it full time.
>
> Anyway, I used to work in customer service at a tire store – that's sort of industrial – so I'm sure your company can benefit from my service-orientation and the fact that if I can deal with irate customers in a tire store, I can sure work with corporate managers about events. People like events a whole lot more than buying tires..."

Get the picture? This event planner wouldn't get a call back. Here are some major mistakes the caller made:

Saying, "I'm Just a Beginner"

I can't think of an instance where you would want to volunteer the fact that you are a beginner. After all, how would you feel about your brain surgeon if he said he was "just a beginner"? Don't see yourself as a rookie, but as an idea person who has the experience and expertise to make things happen for potential clients.

Talking About "Me, Me, Me"

Notice how many times the first caller said "I" or "me." Potential clients, like most other humans, are more interested in their own needs than hearing "me-focused" comments like these.

Burdening Your Potential Client With Your Survival

"My family really needs the money I can make from this" is not an appropriate thing to say to a prospective client. You don't want pity. You want to run a business. You want to serve clients. Tell them what you can do for them, not what you want them to do for you. See yourself as a businessperson exploring whether doing business with this company would be beneficial for both of you.

Communicate your message with confidence. Assume that what you offer is something the decision-maker wants. Assume you can do, with excellence, anything your clients want. Your call is much more likely to be returned if that can-do attitude infects every contact you make with every potential client on the planet.

Instead, here's a much better approach, which can be modified to suit whatever your own specialization is.

> "Hello (first name of potential client), this is Paul Planner. I help companies plan unique special events that delight employees and customers. Please give me a call at 555-1234 so we can discuss how this service would benefit your company."

If your call is intriguing and the company needs event planning services or is looking to improve its customer or employee relationships – as many companies are – your call is likely to get returned. However, there is no way to get appointments with every single person you call, not even if you are Julia Roberts. (Well, unless you say you're from the IRS and have a "serious matter" to discuss.) But failing either of those two things, just be polite and move on if you don't get the response you're seeking. Remember, there is a buyer for every product and service. And you are offering something of value.

How Often Should You Call?

I have heard a few decision-makers say that persistence pays off. In other words, someone who calls repeatedly will eventually get their call returned. However, they are probably the exception to the rule. Most decision-makers say someone who pesters them turns them off. One woman told me she makes a mental note of the people who call repeatedly and resolves never to have anything to do with them.

Calling without leaving a message may seem like a good idea, but many business-people have caller ID on their telephone. If they see a dozen calls from someone who doesn't leave a message, they are likely to assume the caller is selling something they would not be interested in. Not only will the decision-maker not pick up the phone, but also they may become so irritated with the calls that they may respond negatively when the caller finally does leave a message.

If your first call is not returned, I recommend calling a second time a few days later, just in case your first message didn't get through. Messages are rarely erased accidentally, but you wouldn't want to miss a business opportunity if, for some reason, it happened to your call. If neither of your calls is returned, it may be wise to wait awhile before calling again or focus instead on prospective clients who are interested in working with you.

TIP: You are much more likely to get your call returned if you say you were referred by someone the decision-maker knows and respects. Ask for referrals after all your talks and slip "_____ suggested I call you" into the script after your name.

Once You Get Through to the Decision-Maker

Many of the same principles for leaving a message apply when you are speaking directly with the decision-maker. For these calls, you should prepare and practice a script that works well for you. The following is the type of script that has proven to be effective.

YOU: Hello (first name of potential client), this is Paul Planner. I'm calling about an event planning service that can increase sales and enhance employee relations.

TIP: Focus on the benefit that is likely to be of greatest interest to the person you're calling. For example, the Marketing Department is likely to want to "increase sales" while the Human Resources Department will be more interested in a service that can "enhance employee relations."

YOU: (Say lightly, as if the answer is obviously "yes") I'm sure you would say increasing sales and maintaining great employee relations is something (insert name of potential employer's company) cares about, isn't it?

TIP: The decision-maker will respond at this point. Most should respond positively. If he or she doesn't respond positively, you may want to cut the call short and move on to the next name on your list. Trying to turn someone around who won't respond politely to even the most basic question is almost always a waste of time and energy.

YOU: I thought so. My services can help (insert name of company) increase sales and improve employee relations with unique special events that delight employees and customers. I have a 15-minute presentation that explains my services in detail. I'd like to meet with you to show you my portfolio of events I've planned for other companies. Do you have 15 minutes in your schedule on Wednesday afternoon, or might Thursday morning work better for you?

As the example above illustrates, you can avoid a mistake many cold callers make of giving the decision-maker a choice between saying "yes" to a meeting or saying "no." Instead, give them a choice between two possible meeting dates. If you want to set up a meeting, you should also clearly state a time limit – ideally no more than 20 minutes – because many decision-makers view their time as limited.

You may get a nibble right then, and an appointment. Or the decision-maker may ask you to send things to look at before you're offered an appointment. If that's the case, say:

"I'll be happy to do that. If you can switch me back to your assistant, I'll make sure I have the proper mailing information. And if I may, I'll just touch base with you around the middle of next week. Thanks so much, Mr. McOrder."

However, instead of getting an appointment or an invitation to send something, don't be surprised to get at least a mild objection. An excellent way to respond is to agree with how the decision-maker feels and explain that many other people felt exactly the same way until they had a chance to learn more about your program.

CLIENT: We don't have a need for this type of service right now.

YOU: I understand how you feel. Many of my clients felt exactly the same way until I was able to show them how they could benefit from this service. I'd like to show you the same thing. Would Wednesday afternoon work for you, or would Thursday morning be better?

Although you are not giving them any more information, the above statement can be surprisingly effective in getting the client to agree to a meeting. Often the first objection is an automatic reaction, and just a little push can get you in the door. However, if the client wants more information, you can certainly give them more. For example,

CLIENT: We always want to save some money and maintain good client relations, but I'd have to know a little bit more about what you're selling to set up an appointment.

YOU: I understand. In addition to planning memorable events that can help you get more business from your clients, I can show you how to improve employee productivity through company events. Would Wednesday afternoon work for you, or would Thursday morning be better?

If the decision-maker is still not interested, then move on to the next person on your list. If you are overly aggressive, most decision-makers will be turned off and may not want to do business with you. Your time could be better spent focusing on people who are interested in what you have to offer.

Don't worry if your first few calls don't go as planned. Consider them practice. Once you have been using this approach for a while, it should generate a respectable success rate. Depending on what you are proposing, a good success rate for setting up meetings may be one "yes" out of every ten calls or even one "yes" out of every two calls. It is up to you to determine if making a lot of cold calls is a good use of your time.

If this approach doesn't work, go back and take a hard look at your script. Are you clearly communicating the benefits of taking the action you suggest to the decision-maker? If you believe you are, ask someone you respect to listen to you make some of your calls. They may discover something in the way you communicate that could be improved.

Having Someone Phone For You

An alternative to phoning yourself is to have someone phone for you. This can give the impression that you are already an established corporate consulting firm. Like many of us, clients can be influenced by how things appear, and may assume you are a successful professional to have people working for you.

One way to have someone call for you is to hire someone you pay on an hourly or commission basis. This person might work for you full-time or part-time, from your office or from their home. You might find the right person through word of mouth or from a classified ad. In addition to phoning, you might have the person you hire assist you with other tasks as well. (Chapter 5 has more information on hiring employees and contractors.)

Another alternative is to have a friend or relative call on your behalf. Ideally this person should have a **different last name** from yours, or they should simply introduce themselves by their first name. (It doesn't sound nearly as impressive to hear, "Hello, this is Polly Planner calling on behalf of Paul Planner.")

Direct Mail

Other ways to promote your event planning business to corporations include sending letters, brochures, or newsletters to the same people you would contact with cold calls.

According to event planner Lynn Simpson, pictures are especially important to include on all of your letters, brochures and all mailings. People want to see other people having fun at one of your events. Choose your photos carefully — they should represent the very best theme, clientele, and venue that you have to offer a new client.

After your initial contact by mail, follow up with a phone call.

6.4.3 Responding to a Request For Proposal

Government departments and some other corporate employers use an RFP (Request for Proposal) process to select event planners.

As a potential "supplier" of event planning services to government, you would receive a Request for Proposal or RFP. (To be invited to submit a proposal you will first have to ensure government departments and agencies are aware of your services.) When you submit your proposal, you are making a "bid" to do the work.

A typical RFP is a document that provides information about the organization, their needs, the target audience, what they require in a proposal, and specific instructions for submission of the proposal.

You should expect to sell your company's suitability to handle the event, your fees and any other pertinent information. Here is an example of the type of information that might be expected in a proposal:

- A description of your company

- Demonstration of your capability to develop and deliver the event

- A proposed timetable

- A fixed price quotation for development and delivery of the event

- Specific resources (such as employees) that you will assign to the project

- References from organizations you have done similar programs for

- An explanation of how you will measure results

The bid process may also require you to make an oral presentation. The organization requesting the RFP will usually hold a session (sometimes called a bidding meeting) for interested parties (event planners and other suppliers) to attend to learn more about the event before submitting their response to the RFP. This is the time to ask questions and elicit clear answers. The more clearly you understand the goals and purpose of the event, the better your chances of being the successful bidder.

When responding to an RFP, make sure your response gets in before the stated deadline and answers all of the questions accurately. Keep a current personal or company resume on file for these occasions, and don't overstate your qualifications to win a bid.

If you have never planned and organized an international symposium for thousands of attendees, don't make it sound as if you have. Be patient and be prepared to start with smaller events and work your way up to the challenge of this type of event.

Include written references from past events you helped to plan – even ones where you provided a service for free – and include a list of qualifications. Advise them of your availability and make certain you point out exactly what services you will and – more importantly – will not cover.

The client may not be obligated to award the contract to the "lowest cost" bidder. Instead, they may make their decision based on a number of factors, including the event planning company's previous experience presenting similar events.

A number of companies specialize in writing proposals. You can find them by doing a web search for "writing proposals" and "contract." An excellent resource is Deborah Kluge's webpage at **www.proposalwriter.com/links.html** with links on proposal writing and government contracting. Her proposal pointers are great!

Recommended books on proposal writing include *Proven Proposal Strategies to Win More Business*, by Herman Holtz, and *Win Government Contracts for Your Small Business*, by John Di Giacomo and James Kleckner.

6.5 Working With Clients

No matter what marketing techniques you use, you can expect to start getting calls from people interested in using your services. In this section you will find some tips for working with prospective clients and turning them into paying clients.

6.5.1 Responding to Inquiries

Your first contact with some new clients may be over the phone, when they call to ask about your services and prices. Always answer your phone in a professional, friendly voice with your company name.

Do not allow family members to answer your phone if you are not available, and be sure to have your voice mail pick up if you are running after a screaming child and the family dog. A harried response does not make a good first impression of someone who is supposed to stay calm, cool and collected during any crisis.

Have a full packet of your promotional materials on your desk near the phone so you can refer to them, and be sure you don't leave anything out. Also, write down the caller's phone number and address, too, if possible. Then you'll have it and you'll be able to enter it into your database if the caller becomes a customer. And you'll also have it if the caller doesn't immediately become a customer. Enter it into your database with other prospects and e-mail them from time to time. Let them know about special events they might be interested in.

Many of your telephone interviews will be from private citizens searching for information on pricing and services. Many prospective corporate clients already know what an event planner does, so they may be calling to set up an appointment or to send out a Request for Proposal (see section 6.4.3).

Smart businesspeople attempt to set up a face-to-face meeting to discuss their services more in-depth than what a phone call will allow, and you can use this first contact to set up the meeting.

So how can you keep the person on the phone and convince them to meet with you? By gently taking control of the conversation and keeping your answers concise and focused on what a valuable service event planners provide — a stress-free event. Your conversation could go something like this:

> **CLIENT:** Hello, I'm looking for some information on how much you charge to plan an event.
>
> **YOU:** Thank you for calling. My name is Polly Planner. May I get your name?
>
> **CLIENT:** Jane Smith.
>
> **YOU:** Would you prefer if I called you Jane or Ms. Smith?

CLIENT: Call me Jane.

YOU: Well, Jane, our company has many excellent packages and pricing options available, depending on the number of services you want us to handle. We can also design a package especially for you. We're experts at negotiating and securing fair prices from suppliers, and we pass the savings on to you. Have you had a chance to see our portfolio or any information on our company's services?

CLIENT: No. I just got your number from the phone book and thought I'd call. I'm not even sure I understand everything an event planner does.

YOU: Jane, I'm not sure what another event planner would tell you, but I can tell you my goal is to create exciting, stress-free and unique events for my clients. I offer a free one-hour initial consultation and I'd be pleased to meet with you to take the mystery out of what an event planner does and to discuss options with you. I have Tuesday and Thursday evening or Friday afternoon open. Which day would be good for you?

There are many ways to deliver information on your pricing options and services to clients (e-mail, your website, fax, brochures, etc.), but the absolute best way to deliver your information is with a personal meeting.

If Jane Smith decides she'd rather get the information in the mail, send it at once. Make absolutely certain you spell her name correctly and repeat the address back to confirm it. Ask for her phone number for follow-up purposes, mail your materials in an appropriately-sized envelope (don't squish them in), and make sure you use the correct postage. Send a cover letter thanking her for her interest in your company and tell her you will follow up within a few days. Call in a couple of days to ensure she received the materials and ask if she has any questions.

6.5.2 First Meeting with a New Client

The fact that a busy person has agreed to meet with you means they are interested in your services. While there is no guarantee that you will get a particular client or project, if they have a need for your services and are meeting with you, you have a good chance of getting their business.

Where to Meet

If you are fortunate enough to have an office outside your home, and it is a nicely decorated space, by all means have the consultation in your office. You will be close to all of the materials you've gathered during your research and learning stage and you'll be able to answer questions with pictures as well as words.

Similarly, if you have a home office that is nicely decorated and free from interruptions (i.e. no children, barking dogs, etc.), you are licensed to have a home-based business, and the client is comfortable meeting in your home, have the meeting there.

If, on the other hand, you do not have either of these spaces available to you, you should meet at a spot you know will allow you to have a fairly private and uninterrupted conversation. If the event is a private party and the client is comfortable with it, you could have the meeting at their home or in a private room of a restaurant. However, if the event is a corporate event, it would be a good idea to hold the meeting at the client's office.

What to Bring to the Meeting

At the initial consultation, the client will want to see examples of your work, letters of recommendation and any other credentials that would illustrate your ability to plan the client's event — in other words, all of the materials you will have in your prepared portfolio. Here are some additional items an organized event planner would bring to a client meeting:

- Your brochure or other marketing materials

- References from past clients (family or friends included)

- Your business cards

- A two-year calendar or date book that includes the next year

- A blank contract

- A budget estimator spreadsheet

- A calculator

Although this initial consultation may be seen only as an opportunity for the client to assess whether they want to hire you as their event planner, it is a good idea to come prepared to write up a contract.

What to Wear

What you wear to the first meeting should be dictated in part by the type of client you are meeting. For instance, if the meeting is with a large corporation and the event they are planning is a meeting of their board of directors, you should dress in appropriate business attire.

For women, this means darker-colored pants, skirts, and jackets. You can add a funky piece of jewelry, fashionable scarf or dynamite handbag for creativity. Men should wear formal business attire to this type of meeting, meaning a two-piece suit complete with shirt and tie.

If you are meeting with a team of volunteers from that same corporation to plan a company picnic, you can loosen up somewhat — meaning colored suits or separates that are put together well for women, and business casual (suit jacket and pants but no tie) for men. Instead of the typical dress shirt, a man may choose to wear a knitted turtleneck sweater. Having said that, beware that the CFO or CEO of the corporation will still want to meet with you after the volunteers, so don't get too eclectic or faddish in your dress style.

There are a few cases where you can relax the rules a bit. Let's say you have been contacted by a rock band to stage their latest CD release party. Arriving in a black business suit will probably make the group feel uncomfortable. And, while I don't think you should dress like Britney Spears on stage, you can certainly relax the rules and dress a bit more trendy. No matter what type of meeting you are attending, the following rules apply:

- shoes must be absolutely spotless, in good repair (no cracked heels or broken shoelaces) and scuff-free

- do not wear jeans (unless it's event day and the event is a rodeo!)

- don't wear workout gear (tights, lycra, spandex, etc.)

- leave the gum at home (if you absolutely must have something in your mouth try a very small mint or use mouthwash just before the meeting)

Remember what your mother told you: You only have one chance to make a good impression.

Developing a Client Relationship

The fact that this busy person has agreed to meet with you means they are interested in your services. As mentioned above, while there is no guarantee that you will get a particular client or project, if someone has a need for your services and is meeting with you, you have a good chance of getting their business.

Your purpose during this meeting is to turn a prospective client into a client. The way to do this is by identifying what your client needs and wants, so you can communicate how your services will benefit them.

This is where your interpersonal communication skills will really pay off (see section 3.1.1 if this is an area you need to improve). You can begin by giving a quick overview of your services, however, during your meeting you should mostly ask and listen. Aim to have your client do about 80% of the talking. (Of course take your cue from the client. If they prefer not to do a lot of talking, don't try to force it.)

Instead of describing all your services, focus specifically on what the client wants, and offer a few ideas for their event. Don't worry about someone stealing your ideas and then deciding not to use your services. Being willing to share a few innovative ideas will leave the impression that you have many more which you haven't shared.

You should also emphasize the benefits of hiring you. By asking questions, you will likely find that one of the following is a benefit this person would be interested in:

- You can actually save the client money because you can nego-tiate lower prices with suppliers. (This will depend on both your fees and the relationships you have established with suppliers. However, you should definitely let them know that – even after paying your fee – the event will cost less than if they had orga-nized it themselves.)

- You can save the client many hours of time. You could show them the checklist (critical path) of all the details that have to be organized, and ask if they have the time and energy to do all those things on top of their day-to-day busy schedules.

- You can find reputable suppliers and ensure there are no major event "disasters" because you have back-up plans in place for all suppliers and most circumstances.

- The client can enjoy a stress-free event experience.

Remember to focus on what the client wants. Ask them why they are interested in hiring an event planner, and what they think you can do for them. In answering these questions, they may talk themselves into hiring you!

A Final Note

No matter how your meeting goes – whether you end up with a client or not – a thank you note is important. If the meeting did result in a client, you need to thank the person for that. If it didn't, you need to thank the person for his or her time, and be sure to tell them you are available to serve them when they do decide to shift the task of plan-ning an event to you. Plus, even if they are not ready, it gives them a chance to mention to their friends who need an event planner "Hey, I know someone you could hire ..."

After your meeting, make sure you follow up with the client. Decisions can take time, especially when a committee is involved, but keeping in touch ensures the client keeps you in mind.

When you get the good news that a client wants to work with you, that's when you'll be putting other parts of this guide to use. You'll need to send out a contract (see chapter 5) and actually plan the event (see chapter 2).

Bonus Tips to Market Your Business

The nature of people is the same — it is their habits that separate them. As the saying goes, "Successful people are willing to do what unsuccessful people are not."

When you own your own event planning business, you must believe in the potential success of that business — and you must believe in yourself 100 percent. But believing in something is not the same as succeeding. You must commit all your time, effort, money, energy, skill and stamina in order for your business to become a success. Spend a little time truthfully reassessing whether your habits reflect a successful or unsuccessful business owner – and then commit to making the changes in your habits that will ensure success.

Professionals in the event planning/meeting planning industry Marcia Bradley, Sherri Brennan and Lynn Simpson share some of their tips on how to market and develop your own event planning business:

- Be passionate about your business and its future

- Cultivate a personal mentor — an experienced person in the industry

- Offer work pro bono (volunteer) — at least one project per year

- Know your competition

- Learn to listen more than you talk

- Find your niche and be the best

- Give and get at least one business card every day

- Develop two new event services each year

- Recycle information — pass along event leads you can't use to others in the field

- Make three cold calls every day

- Remain open to joint ventures and possible merges

- Offer a free newsletter for event planners through your web site

- Form a local chapter of event planners

- Be highly visible in your community

- Hold event planning seminars, host programs, write manuals and speak

- Take care of your physical health

- Surround yourself with positive employees

- Throw an open house once each year — it's a great chance to show off your planning expertise

7. Appendix

7.1 Professional Associations

There are many associations offering information for event planners. Some also offer training, certification, and job listings. Visit the websites of the following organizations to see what they can offer you. Other organizations are listed in chapter 4 and throughout the guide.

- *American Hotel & Lodging Association*
  www.ahma.com

- *American Society of Association Executives (ASAE)*
  www.asaenet.org

- *Canadian Special Events Society*
  www.cses.ca/index.html

- *CanadianSpecialEvents.com*
  www.canadianspecialevents.com

- *Convention Industry Council (CIC)*
  www.conventionindustry.org

- *Hospitality Sales & Marketing Association*
  www.hsmai.org

- *International Society of Meeting Planners (ISMP)*
  www.iami.org/ismp.cfm

- *International Special Events Society (ISES)*
  www.ises.com

- *Meeting Professionals International (MPI)*
  www.mpiweb.org

7.2 Periodicals

- *Event Solutions*
  www.event-solutions.com

- *Special Events*
  www.specialevents.com

- *Corporate Meetings & Incentives*
  http://cmi.meetingsnet.com

- *Meeting News*
  www.meetingnews.com

- *Meetings & Conventions*
  www.meetings-conventions.com

- *Successful Meetings*
  www.successmtgs.com

7.3 Message Boards

- *Event Planning Meetup*
  http://eventplanning.meetup.com

- *Meeting Planners Message Board*
  www.mmaweb.com/meetings/meetingboard

- *Yahoo! Groups: Event Planning*
  http://groups.yahoo.com/search?query=event+planning